Cambridge Elements

Elements in the Philosophy of Friedrich Nietzsche
edited by
Kaitlyn Creasy
California State University, San Bernardino
Matthew Meyer
The University of Scranton

NIETZSCHE'S REVALUATION OF ALL VALUES

Thomas H. Brobjer
Uppsala University

CAMBRIDGE
UNIVERSITY PRESS

CAMBRIDGE
UNIVERSITY PRESS

Shaftesbury Road, Cambridge CB2 8EA, United Kingdom

One Liberty Plaza, 20th Floor, New York, NY 10006, USA

477 Williamstown Road, Port Melbourne, VIC 3207, Australia

314–321, 3rd Floor, Plot 3, Splendor Forum, Jasola District Centre,
New Delhi – 110025, India

103 Penang Road, #05–06/07, Visioncrest Commercial, Singapore 238467

Cambridge University Press is part of Cambridge University Press & Assessment,
a department of the University of Cambridge.

We share the University's mission to contribute to society through the pursuit of
education, learning and research at the highest international levels of excellence.

www.cambridge.org
Information on this title: www.cambridge.org/9781009539470

DOI: 10.1017/9781009421652

First published 2024

A catalogue record for this publication is available from the British Library

ISBN 978-1-009-53947-0 Hardback
ISBN 978-1-009-42163-8 Paperback
ISSN 2976-5722 (online)
ISSN 2976-5714 (print)

Nietzsche's Revaluation of All Values

Elements in the Philosophy of Friedrich Nietzsche

DOI: 10.1017/9781009421652
First published online: November 2024

Thomas H. Brobjer
Uppsala University

Author for correspondence: Thomas H. Brobjer, Thomas.Brobjer@idehist.uu.se

Abstract: Why is Nietzsche's thought and philosophy still regarded as relevant today? There are a large number of possible answers to a question like this, but one of the most important and persuasive is that Nietzsche questioned and discussed the nature, character and value of our values. Nietzsche frequently turns other questions such as epistemological and ontological ones into axiological ones, making values pivotal in his thought. It is possible to argue that the revaluation of all values is both the most important and today the most relevant of Nietzsche's main philosophical themes and projects. Furthermore, the theme is intimately involved with what Nietzsche regarded as his most important work, his magnum opus (that he called his *Hauptwerk*), for a long period called *The Will to Power* but later *Revaluation of All Values*.

Keywords: Nietzsche, Revaluation of Values, axiology, values, magnum opus

ISBNs: 9781009539470 (HB), 9781009421638 (PB), 9781009421652 (OC)
ISSNs: 2976-5722 (online), 2976-5714 (print)

Contents

1 Revaluation of All Values as a Philosophical Project

Nietzsche uses the expression 'revaluation of all values' in two different, but for him related, senses. On the one hand, it refers to a philosophical task or problem related to the setting of rank of values and the determination of the value of values. On the other hand, he used it as the title (at first as subtitle) to his planned philosophical magnum opus in four volumes that he worked on from at least 1884 until his collapse, but never completed. The first time Nietzsche ever used the expression was as a subtitle to that work. I have here separated these aspects, and in the first part treat it as a philosopheme and in the second part as a literary project.

1.1 Introduction to Section 1: Revaluation of Values as a Philosophical Project

Why is Nietzsche's thought and philosophy still regarded as relevant today? There are a large number of possible answers to a question like this, but one of the most important and persuasive is that Nietzsche questioned and discussed the nature, character, and value of our values. Nietzsche frequently turns other questions such as epistemological and ontological ones into axiological ones, making values pivotal in his thought. It is possible to argue that the revaluation of all values is both the most important and today the most relevant of Nietzsche's main philosophical themes and projects. Furthermore, the theme is intimately involved with what Nietzsche regarded as his most important work, his magnum opus (that he called his *Hauptwerk*), for a long period called *The Will to Power* but later *Revaluation of All Values*.

Revaluation of all values, the critique of Christian and modern values, and the affirmation of an alternative set of values are generally regarded as one of Nietzsche's most important main themes or tropes. Nietzsche refers to the expression for the first time in his published books in *Beyond Good and Evil* (BGE 46), and it is therefore usually regarded as a late trope, as important during the last years, 1886–88. I will show that it began much earlier, including that it is important in *Thus Spoke Zarathustra* (1883–85), where, surprisingly, it is usually ignored, probably because he does not yet use the word 'revaluation'. I instead argue that its origin should be regarded as occurring in 1880/81. I thereafter comment on its rather complex context at this time, with no single obvious thematic textual context outweighing all the others. I will also consider some of the consequences of this early dating.

Relatively little interest has been directed at Nietzsche's revaluation of all values by philosophers and scholars. This is surprising considering the import-ance the late Nietzsche gives to it and unfortunate since a disregard of it is associated with an overemphasis on Nietzsche's critical philosophy at the price of undervaluing his constructive and affirmative alternative. In *Ecce Homo* (EH BGE 1 and EH Destiny 1), he suggests that the revaluation is the goal and purpose of his life.

The revaluation of all values consists of a critique of our present and Christian values and an affirmation of another set of healthier values. What some of these alternative values can be I will mention herein. The expression 'revaluation' started as a planned subtitle, later the full title, of what Nietzsche regarded as his most important work, his magnum opus (*Hauptwerk*).

I will next show that (a) Nietzsche speaks of the revaluation in terms of a dichotomy of values – in terms of the existence of two paradigms of values; (b) one revaluation has already occurred, from antiquity to modernity by the means of Socrates, Plato, and Christianity; (c) a second 'opposite' revaluation has been attempted during the Renaissance but failed: the 'Renaissance [. . .] The revaluation of Christian values [. . .] *my* question is its question', and (d) that Nietzsche explicitly denies utopian interpretations of the revaluation and affirms the importance of history for the revaluation: 'I sought in history the beginning of the construction of the reverse ideals (the concepts "pagan", "classical", "noble" newly discussed and expounded –).' Nietzsche also gives some other more specific clues to his own revaluation. (e) He reverses the conventional moral statement 'do this and you will be happy' by claiming instead 'a "happy one" *must* perform certain acts', i.e., that character determines actions. (f) He also refers to his first book (*The Birth of Tragedy*) and its attempt to revive tragedy as part of his revaluation: 'Everything in this essay is prophetic: the proximity of the return of the Greek spirit, the necessity for *counter Alexanders* to *retie* the Gordian knot of Greek culture after it had been untied.' Finally, with his very strong person-oriented approach, (g) he claims that '*we ourselves*, we free spirits, are already a "revaluation of all values"'.

Important for understanding the revaluation is that Nietzsche constructs a dichotomy of values. The very explicit use of such expressions as 'reversing ideals', 'the opposite values', 'antithetical evaluations' 'stand evaluations *on their head*', 'inimical value', and 'the *inverse* values' clearly indicates that there basically exist only two alternatives. Most emphasis is by Nietzsche placed on ancient contra Christian values which are seen, for example, by his recurrent claim that the present values have ruled for two millennia, but many other versions of essentially the same dichotomy are also mentioned: master-morality contra slave-morality, noble contra plebeian, Roman contra Jewish, and moralities of self-affirmation contra self-denial. At least one revaluation has already occurred in the history of European culture, and Socrates, Plato, Jesus, and Paul are associated with this, and Luther with its revival. Many of Nietzsche's statements imply that the revaluation will mean an inversion of values so that the values held in low esteem today will be held in high, and conversely. Furthermore, the present Christian values are regarded as anti-natural. On several occasions, Nietzsche implies that the revaluation has already begun, and even occurred, through Nietzsche himself and his equals. It follows that Nietzsche's affirmative values are the values associated with the healthy side of the dichotomy. Finally, we are in fact given an example of a revaluation from decadence to health in the form of the Renaissance, and Nietzsche closely associates the present revaluation to that of the Renaissance – '*my* question is its question'.

Apart from these general statements, we are also given three concrete examples of what Nietzsche means by the revaluation. First, he refers to his understanding of Greek tragedy as his first revaluation of all values: 'the soil out of which I draw all that I will and *can*'. Second, he claims that the free spirits already constitute a revaluation of all values. Furthermore, Nietzsche ends *Ecce Homo* with the statement: '*Dionysus against the Crucified*', where Dionysus represents healthy and life-affirming values, while the Crucified represents Christian and present values.

1.2 The Interpretation of the Revaluation in Secondary Literature

Surprisingly, studies of the revaluation of all values remain remarkably rare. This is evident from both bibliographies and the discussions in many book-length studies of Nietzsche. Many books on Nietzsche discuss will to power, *Übermensch*, and eternal recurrence, but say nothing, or almost nothing, about the revaluation of all values. Others say little. Some examples: Karl Jaspers seems to understand it as the creation of essentially wholly new values. Tracy Strong, in his interesting study, has two long chapters on the will to power and the eternal return, little about the *Übermensch* but no chapter on the revaluation, and, in spite of a very detailed index, no entry corresponding to revaluation. Thiele emphasizes the transvaluation as the creation of new values after the old ones have been destroyed (nihilism). Schutte, who has written a PhD on the revaluation, seems to hold a similar view in *Beyond Nihilism: Nietzsche without Masks* (1986). Philippa Foot, in her 'Nietzsche: The Revaluation of Values', published in Solomon (1973, 1980), emphasizes the critical nature of the revaluation as an attack on Christian and 'all morality'.

Walter Kaufmann (1974) has a long chapter in his book on Nietzsche entitled 'The Death of God and the Revaluation' (also republished separately in Solomon). However, the actual discussion of the revaluation covers only eight pages. Kaufmann asks if Nietzsche offers us new values, or, expressed

differently, if it is his intention to pour us new wine: 'The answer is: No. [...]
In other words, the "revaluation" was a war against accepted valuations, not
the creation of new values' (1974: 111). The revaluation is 'the diagnosis itself'.
However, strangely enough, Kaufmann adds that 'this consists in nothing
beyond what Socrates did', referring to Socrates in his role as a 'gadfly' and
quoting Nietzsche's use of him in this sense. This is unfortunate, for Nietzsche
also regarded Socrates as one of the most important revaluators of the first
negative revaluation, the one from antiquity to moralization and Christianity.
Kaufmann's conclusion is clearly that the revaluation is a critical project: 'The
revaluation is thus the alleged discovery that our morality is, *by its own stand-
ards*, poisonously immoral' (1974: 113). However, he also mentions, but without drawing conclusions or consequences, that 'The "revaluation" is not a new
value-legislation but reverses prevalent valuations that reversed ancient valuations' (1974: 111).

Ackermann's book *Nietzsche: A Frenzied Look* is one which attempts 'to
sketch Nietzsche in movement' in which much of Nietzsche's later thought is
related back to his earlier writings and to his sympathy with the pre-Socratics.
Without going into details, he nonetheless claims in the preface: 'I try to show
Nietzsche's thoughts develop and ramify from his early, concentrated vision of
Greece before Socrates, a vision that Nietzsche never abandons and a vision that
is the source of his shocking new tables of values' (1989: ix).

One work that does take the 'revaluation of all values' as a central thought in
Nietzsche's philosophy is Beat Kissling's 400-page PhD dissertation entitled
Die Umwertung der Werte als Pädagogisches Projekt Nietzsches (1992). It also
acknowledges the importance of early Greek thought for Nietzsche, but the
emphasis in the book is on interpretations of Nietzsche's views by later thinkers,
and on its relevance for pedagogics.

This general lack of discussions about the revaluation is surprising and
unfortunate. It is surprising, considering Nietzsche's own emphasis, which is
as much, or more, on this theme as on any other. It is unfortunate, since this is
closely associated with Nietzsche's own affirmative or constructive values. A
disregard of the revaluation is associated with an over-emphasis on Nietzsche's
critical philosophy at the price of under-valuating his constructive and affirmative alternative. It is also 'unfortunate' because we are confused about and lack
understanding of values, and Nietzsche is one of the few philosophers who have
thought profoundly about values.

A work that frequently mentions revaluation is Bernard Reginster's *The
Affirmation of Life: Nietzsche on Overcoming Nihilism* (2006), where his main
claim is the truism that according to Nietzsche, for us to overcome nihilism, we
need to revalue the values that leads to nihilism (50). Reginster uses a rather

analytical approach and divides nihilism into two forms, nihilism of despair and nihilism of disorientation (a dichotomy that Nietzsche does not set up). He assumes that Nietzsche regarded that 'the essential inhospitality of this world' leads to despair (100). However, Nietzsche seems to regard life-affirmation as being natural (and therefore refers to natural and anti-natural, i.e., decadent, values), especially before the first revaluation (performed by the Jews, Christianity, and Plato). Nietzsche emphasizes the richness and superabundance of life, nature, and the world. He thus, counter to Reginster, regards affirmation as the default view (Nietzsche rejects pessimism as well as nihilism). Nowhere does the book discuss or even mention the first 'negative' revaluation nor the four-volume literary project, *Revaluation of All Values*, that Nietzsche worked hard on for the last four to five years of his active life. Reginster bases much of his arguments on the somewhat unreliable collection of late notes, *The Will to Power*, rather than on the much more reliable KSA (which also is much more chronologically reliable).

A full-length study of Nietzsche's revaluation is E. E. Sleinis' *Nietzsche's Revaluation of Values: A Study in Strategies* (1994). His emphasis is 'on the theoretical feasibility of such an enterprise'. His main concern is to examine the apparently impossible attempt to revalue all values. Can values be revalued without recourse to values? For this purpose, he examines the methods and strategies Nietzsche uses. He argues that Nietzsche has a naturalistic conception of value and that the source of all value lies within valuing beings. Further, he asserts that for Nietzsche there exists an objective measure of value and that this is power. In four chapters, he deals with truth, moral values, religious values, and aesthetic values, and their relation to a revaluation. For example, in the chapter on religious values, Sleinis correctly argues that Nietzsche performs a meta-revaluation in that he views religions not as an ontological thesis but as essentially concerned with value. Concretely, he argues that Nietzsche's higher-order values are those that result in the invigoration and the enrichment of life.

This book thus contains both more and less than its title seems to promise. There is no examination of what Nietzsche said or meant when he referred to revaluation, nor any discussions of the concrete values that Nietzsche referred to as healthy values. What it does contain is an analytical account of much of Nietzsche's philosophy in general and especially regarded values. However, the gap between what Nietzsche actually says and Sleinis' analysis is often so great that the analysis becomes less interesting and all too abstract. Nowhere in the book is there any reference to, or discussion of, Nietzsche's many statements that a revaluation has already occurred between antiquity and Christianity. These and many other of Nietzsche's references to revaluation give us important information about what Nietzsche meant by revaluation. To me, it seems very clear that it is not an abstract revaluation of all our present values, including all of Nietzsche's own values, into something completely new. Instead, the revaluation refers to the change from one set of (life-denying) values to another and opposing set of (life-affirming) values. Some of these values will be new, but many will be old in the sense that we are aware of them today and that they were even more prevalent during antiquity and the Renaissance. With such a view, many of Sleinis' investigations appear abstract and irrelevant, but a number of side issues are clarified and his examination of many of Nietzsche's strategies remains relevant and illuminating. A related study is Aaron Ridley's article 'Nietzsche and the Re-Evaluation of Values' (2005) that also, in an analytical manner, attempts to clarify what a revaluation would entail. Both studies conclude that a revaluation is at least theoretically feasible.

John Richardson has recently written a valuable study, *Nietzsche's Values* (2020), that contains many interesting and good arguments and insights. Especially valuable, it seems to me, is his emphasis on value, on truth, and on using historical approaches. However, oddly enough, revaluation is not much discussed in the book. There is no chapter or subchapter that discusses it, nor does he refer to the only full book-length study of revaluation, that of Sleinis (discussed earlier), and in the index the term 'Revaluation' has only five pages listed, and these pages do not contain much discussion of it. He, like a better Sleinis, works mostly on a theoretical level. There is little discussion of actual values Nietzsche revalues, and there is no discussion or even mention of the four-volume literary project, *Revaluation of All Values*, that Nietzsche worked on. Nonetheless, Richardson correctly points out that 'genealogy is indispensable for a *revaluation* of our values' (325) because it discloses the origin of our values and because it creates a necessary distancing effect that history always has. He further argues that what Nietzsche wants is 'spiritual' growth, not a technological, an economic or one of physical power, but 'understanding of itself and especially of its own willing and valuing' (456). He continues:

> What Nietzsche anticipates, I suggest, is another advance in human self-awareness, comparable to that by which human passed from 'custom' into 'morality' [. . .] it will happen at the whole societal level: new capacities will be trained into members generally via new shared norms. These new norms will be the outcome of the '*revaluation of values*' Nietzsche so famously calls for (456).

He further points out that 'the overall way Nietzsche means to "revalue" our norms is by "de-moralizing" them' (457). These, and many other observations, are valuable, but it seems to over-emphasize the social and long-term aspects of a revolution of values, and miss the more concrete revaluations (e.g., of

Christian and moral values) Nietzsche most frequently argues for, and his claims, at least in part, to already have performed.

Andreas Urs Sommer has in his *Friedrich Nietzsches 'Der Antichrist'* (2000) insightfully discussed several aspects of the theme revaluation, and especially emphasized Nietzsche's use of false coinage and fraudulence, e.g., in *The Antichrist*, 12, for references to those who argue for the false present values (from the perspective of the healthy and true early values). He argues that one of the senses of the hammer, in the subtitle of *Twilight of the Idols*, is a 'Prägehammer', which determines which coins are valid and which are false. 'Nietzsche's revaluation reinstalls that, which due to the "false coinage" of the idealists, Christians and other bad company had been regarded as invalid coinage' (155). Joseph Kranak has written an interesting dissertation entitled *Nietzsche's Revaluation of All Values* (Marquette University, 2014), that examines many different aspects of Nietzsche's philosopheme as an unfinished concept (and unfinished work), but without using any German language material.

Much remains to be studied to better understand Nietzsche's revaluation and his views of and relation to value. Perhaps it is also possible for us to use Nietzsche to better understand values and evaluation in general. In a note at the end of the first essay of *On the Genealogy of Morals* (GM I 17, Nietzsche's note), he writes, '*All* the sciences have from now on to prepare the way for the future task of the philosophers: this task understood as the solution of the *problem of value*, the determination of the *order of rank among values*.'

1.3 The Nature, Importance, and Meaning of the 'Revaluation of All Values'

The importance for Nietzsche of the revaluation was great. From *Beyond Good and Evil* (BGE 46 and 203), where it is explicitly introduced in his published writings, it constitutes an outstanding *Leitmotif*, and it reaches a crescendo in the last books, promising even more for the near future. In *Ecce Homo,* he seems to suggest that the revaluation is the goal and purpose of his life. The *Leitmotif* is so strong that it is reflected in most of the book titles from *Beyond Good and Evil* onwards. *Beyond Good and Evil* means beyond our present and Christian moral values (but not beyond good and bad), and the subtitle, *Prelude to a Philosophy of the Future*, seems to point to the future epoch with new values Nietzsche hopes we will enter, as well as to his planned magnum opus in four volumes, which he had announced as a work in progress on the back cover of the book. The revaluation of all values includes aesthetical values, but since the strongest values today are moral values, the centre of gravity concerns a revaluation of these. Nietzsche, as a philologist, historian, and realist, believes that a revaluation will only succeed if we understand the power and genesis of present values. In this sense, *On the Genealogy of Morals* is a preparatory study for the revaluation. This is also how Nietzsche describes the three essays that constitute the book in *Ecce Homo* after having stated that Christianity is 'a counter-movement, the great revolt against the domination of *noble* values' and that it was born out of a spirit of *ressentiment*: 'Three decisive preliminary studies of a psychologist for a revaluation of all values' (EH 'Books' GM). Though not obvious from the title, *The Case of Wagner* concerns a revaluation of aesthetic values, mainly in the sense parallel to *Beyond Good and Evil* and *The Antichrist*, i.e., in the form of a critique of the decadent values of which Wagner is 'the most instructive case'.[1] Or as he says in the discussion of the work in *Ecce Homo*: '*What* is it I suffer from when I suffer from the destiny of music? From this: that music has been deprived of its world-transfiguring, affirmative character, that it is *décadence* music and no longer the flute of Dionysus' (EH 'Books' CW:1). The title of the next work, *Twilight of the Idols* (*Götzen-Dämmerung*), stands for a testing and smashing of idols – i.e., of old truths and values, and that these truths and values are on their way out. He presents the book in *Ecce Homo* with the words:

> Anyone who wants to get a quick idea of how topsy-turvy everything was before I came along should make a start with this work. What the title page calls *idol* is quite simply what till now has been called 'truth'. *Twilight of the Idols* – in plain words: the old truth is coming to an end. (EH 'Books' TI:1)

The Antichrist indicates Nietzsche's severe opposition towards Christianity (in all its forms). The subtitle of this work was while he wrote the book and for some time thereafter: *Attempt at a Critique of Christianity. Book One of the Revaluation of All Values*. In the preface to his last original book, Nietzsche explains that the reason for writing *Ecce Homo* was to avoid mistakes as to whom he is, considering that he will soon make the heaviest demand that has ever been made on mankind, i.e., the revaluation, to revalue their values.

---

[1] For aesthetic values, as is also the case in regard to moral values, the healthy values are the classical ones. This is most evident in the epilogue to *The Case of Wagner*: "In its measure of strength every age also possesses a measure for what virtues are permitted and forbidden to it. Either it has the virtues of *ascending* life: then it will resist from the profoundest depths the virtues of declining life. Or the age itself represents declining life: then it also requires the virtues of decline, then it hates everything that justifies itself solely out of abundance, out of the overflowing riches of strength. Aesthetics is tied indissolubly to these biological presuppositions: there is an aesthetics of *decline*, and there is a *classical* aesthetics." The same distinction is discussed in GS, V, 370 (and reprinted in *Nietzsche contra Wagner*) under the title: "*What is romanticism?*" where he makes the main distinction regarding all aesthetical values concerning whether "it is hunger or superabundance that has here become creative?" The values associated with an over-fullness of life are repeatedly referred to as Dionysian.

Since at least 1884 (but really already from 1881), Nietzsche had planned to write a major magnum opus, that he called his *Hauptwerk*, from 1886 using the expression 'revaluation of all values' either in the title or in the subtitle, as I will discuss in Section 2 of this Element. *The Antichrist* was the first and the only finished volume of this *Hauptwerk*, but his notebooks contain plans and notes for the three following volumes.

1.3.1 Four Possible Interpretations of the Meaning of the Revaluation of Values

What is the meaning of the expression 'revaluation of all values'?[2] Two evident preliminary facts can be established. First, the values to be 'revalued' are our present values, whether they be called Christian, modern, nihilistic or European. Second, there has already, according to Nietzsche, been at least one revaluation previously in history, between antiquity and Christianity. This will become more evident as we go into more detail. However, the revaluation is still open to a number of different interpretations:

1. The first interpretation understands the revaluation as a transvaluation of old values to something *new*, i.e., the ancient values were transvalued by Christianity and Christian values are now to be transvalued into something new, fundamentally different from both ancient and Christian values. Such a transvaluation can be regarded as either linear or as being more or less dialectic and Hegelian. This form of interpretation is likely to be somewhat 'utopian' since it will be unable to say much about what these new values are, apart from being new and different, and will probably concentrate on the critical side of the revaluation, but still insisting on the existence of new possibilities. This interpretation is probably also the most common interpretation in general. I will refer to this as the *utopian interpretation*.

2. The second interpretation emphasizes the questioning, the examining, and the diagnosis of values. It argues that the revaluation project is an extension of Nietzsche's statement in *The Gay Science* 269: '*In what do you believe? –* In this, that the weights of all things must be determined anew.*' This

---

[2] Sometimes *Umwerthung* is translated, less accurately, as transvaluation. This translation is less suitable since the meaning of *Umwerthung* for Nietzsche is closer to revaluation than to transvaluation, as will be shown next. This is also shown by the synonyms which he uses for *Umwerthung*, such as *Umkehrung* (= reversal) and *umkehren* (= turn back) and *Umdrehung* (= turn, revolution, rotation) and *umdrehen* (= turn round, turn over, turn back). Finally, considering that Nietzsche was no stranger to the coining of words and phrases, it seems likely that he would have coined the words *Transwerthung* and *transwerthen* if transvaluation was what he meant.

interpretation, which can be called the *critical interpretation*, has even less to say about the future revalued values and hence also about Nietzsche's affirmative values.

3. The third interpretation understands the revaluation as a *reversal* of values, today's high values will after the revaluation become low values and the low ones high. This interpretation can be called a *reversal interpretation*. It implies that the new values are defined in terms of a reversal of *the present values*. It can find support in the texts of Nietzsche but remains problematic since it is rarely obvious what the opposite of most values are without some other measure or criterion. This interpretation is probably unusual, at least among Nietzsche scholars. Some of those critical of Nietzsche's philosophy may hold this view.

4. The fourth interpretation understands the revaluation as essentially a *re*-valuation, i.e., back to earlier ancient, noble, and healthy values. This interpretation is the only one with a fairly clear view of what the new values should be like – with similarity and kinship to the old ancient values – and is thus perhaps more open to falsification than the other three. This interpretation can be called a *dichotomy interpretation* for it assumes that there exist two value-paradigms, the noble and natural contra the anti-natural and decadent, the ancient contra the modern (Christian). This view has often been a minor supplement to the utopian and critical interpretations, but rarely defended as the main interpretation.

It is unlikely that any one of these four interpretations, as ideal types, will alone yield a complete and perfect interpretation. Rather, each of them has its own virtues and strengths and a certain degree of mixture is to be expected. Nonetheless, there are strong arguments that the last, the dichotomy interpretation, is superior to the others.

The dichotomy interpretation does not assume a complete copying of Greek values, only that there are two opposing sets of fundamental values. A copying of values would be both undesirable and impossible (compare KSA 8, 7[1]: 'A culture, which copies a Greek one, can create nothing new'). There is an important ingredient of something new and something different that possibly is understated in its name. This can be seen in Nietzsche's emphasis on creativity, on the new, and on the future.

The supporters of the utopian interpretation make use of a section in *Twilight of the Idols*:

> *In the ear of the Conservatives.* – What was formerly not known, what is known today or could be known – a *reversion*, a turning back in any sense and to any degree, is quite impossible. We physiologists at least know that. But all

priests and moralists have believed it was possible – they have *wanted* to take mankind back, *force* it back, to an *earlier* standard of virtue. Morality has always been a bed of Procrustes. (TI 'Expeditions of an Untimely Man' 43)

This appears to strongly favour the 'utopian' interpretation, or at least falsify the 'reversed' and the 'dichotomy' interpretations. However, this is not the case. Such an understanding of this statement would be comparable to viewing Nietzsche's critique of liberal theologians and free thinkers such as David Strauss as indicating that Nietzsche was a Christian. His view is rather that the conservative and the free thinker are not radical enough. They remain within one value-paradigm and either dilute these values or attempt to return to older outlived versions of the same values. A few sections below in *Twilight of the Idols*, Nietzsche again makes a statement that at first appears to confirm the 'utopian' interpretation but, after closer inspection, actually fits the dichotomy interpretation better.

Progress in my sense. – I too speak of a 'return to nature', although it is not really a going-back but a *going-up* – up into a high, free, even frightful nature and naturalness, such as plays with great tasks, is *permitted* to play with them. (TI 'Expeditions' 48)

Nietzsche immediately adds that 'Napoleon was a piece of "return to nature" as I understand it' and Nietzsche regarded Napoleon as a continuation of the Renaissance. In the following section Goethe is given as another 'return to nature' and also connected with the Renaissance, with healthy values: 'through a going-*up* to the naturalness of the Renaissance' (TI 'Expeditions' 49). Thus, rather than being 'utopian', Nietzsche is concrete and historical and he has no problem referring to the Greeks as an example and as remaining 'the *supreme cultural event* of history – they knew, they *did* what was needed to be done' – i.e., inaugurate culture in the body, *not* the 'soul' (TI 'Expeditions' 47).

Obviously, Nietzsche is primarily concerned with the present or future revaluation. However, many of his discussions and references are to the earlier 'negative' revaluation from antiquity to Christianity. Such an emphasis would be inconsistent with an interpretation of the revaluation as a transvaluation into something new or as mainly being a critique of present values, or at least be rather irrelevant in view of these interpretations. However, this emphasis is wholly consistent with the 'dichotomy' interpretation, and in its light very relevant. The 'utopian' interpretation ignores both the explicit statements Nietzsche makes as to the importance of history – recall his critique of philosophers for their lack of historical sense (TI 'Reason' 1) – and the many specific historical examples Nietzsche gives and uses. In the epilogue to *The Case of Wagner,* he lists as examples of noble morality and master morality: Roman, pagan, classical, Renaissance, and the Icelandic saga. The 'utopian' interpretations are forced to deny the dichotomy of values since they must assume at least a third alternative for the future. Considering the prominent place of the dichotomy in Nietzsche's discussions of the revaluation, this is a very serious flaw. This denial also means that they are forced to interpret Nietzsche's references to the reversal of values much more metaphorically than they are intended. They also ignore the hints that the revaluation already has occurred, with Nietzsche and his equals. In conclusion, this means that they ignore or under-value many of Nietzsche's most fundamental affirmative values associated with, for example, tragedy, antiquity, the Renaissance, and nobility.

The 'critical' interpretation is correct in discussing the critique of our present values. In the preface to *On the Genealogy of Morals* Nietzsche writes: 'Let us articulate this *new demand*: we need a *critique* of moral values, *the value of these values themselves must first be called in question* [. . .] One has taken the *value* of these "values" as given, as factual, as beyond all question' (GM 'Pref' 6). Our present values are, according to Nietzsche, anti-natural and there is a sense in which a critique of these values is likely to lead to a return to natural values, i.e., noble values, like those of the Greeks and the Renaissance. However, in the absence of affirmative values, such critique could also lead to a deepened nihilism or, as was the case with Luther's criticism, to a revival. However, not only does the critical interpretation ignore Nietzsche's affirmative values, but it also ignores or rejects the dichotomy, and this gives its critique of the present values a false perspective. It exchanges the utopian aspects of the previous interpretation for an overly critical interpretation. In ignoring the constructive side of the revaluation, they lay themselves open to Nietzsche's critique: 'Those are my enemies: they want to overthrow but not to build up. They say: "all that is without value" – but do not want to create any value' (KSA 10, 5[1], 218). In what it ignores, the 'critical' interpretation has the same flaws as the previous one.

The third interpretation, which regards the revaluation as a reversal of today's values, is based on Nietzsche's many references to a reversion and inversion of values, and on his critique of our present values. However, this interpretation makes little sense unless one accepts a dichotomy of values, for the meaning of a reversal of values generally, without a dichotomy, is not obvious. The second problem with this interpretation is that it starts with today's values and attempts to invert them. This is a reactive response that fails to take Nietzsche's affirmative ideals into sufficient consideration. When this is done, the interpretation becomes similar to the fourth one, the 'dichotomy' interpretation.

We have seen that the 'dichotomy' interpretation is the one most compatible with Nietzsche's statements regarding the revaluation of all values. However, the revaluation need not be regarded as a *return* to earlier values, for Nietzsche's view is probably better described as claiming that there exist two systems of value – life- and reality-affirming and life- and reality-denying – always and independently of history.[3] However, it remains true that the greatest example of a life-affirming epoch is that of the early Greeks and that we have much to learn from them. There need not be any contradiction between Nietzsche's praise of antiquity and his emphasis on creating values. A large part of the emphasis on the creation of values is directed against merely obeying present values, and choosing values is part of the creation of values. When Nietzsche talks of Greece as a prototype and example, he is not referring to a slavish copying, but to a creative inspiration.

1.3.2 The Meaning of Revaluation in Nietzsche's Books and Notes

Already by the first occurrence of the word revaluation and of the concept 'revaluation of all values' in Nietzsche's published writings, *Beyond Good and Evil* 46, he clearly sets up a dichotomy and claims that a revaluation has already occurred. The dichotomy is between freedom, pride, and self-confidence on one side and enslavement, self-mockery, and self-mutilation on the other, where the latter is associated with Christianity. Then Nietzsche states: 'the paradoxical formula "god on the cross" [...] promised a revaluation of all the values of antiquity' (BGE 46), a dichotomy between ancient and Christian values is constructed. He continues by pointing at the psychology behind the revaluation: slave-natures with 'the great *hidden* suffering' (BGE 46), i.e., resentment at those more privileged than themselves, like the Jews against the Roman nobility with their tolerance. Thus, in this first occurrence, the revaluation referred to is the earlier and *negative* one from antiquity to Christianity. The second reference to the concept, in *Beyond Good and Evil* 203, now refers to a positive revaluation:

> whither must *we* direct our hopes? Towards *new philosophers*, we have no other choice; towards spirits strong and original enough to make a start on antithetical evaluations and to revalue and reverse 'eternal values' [...] a revaluation of values under whose novel pressure and hammer a conscience would be steeled, a heart transformed to brass, so that it might endure the weight of such a responsibility.

Those who are to carry it out would have to be healthy, strong, and hard but it is still not clear what this revaluation would entail. The emphasis still concerns a critique of the present set of 'Christian-European' values, which has led, and leads to an ever-greater diminution of man. However, in the previous section, Nietzsche defined modern morality in the terms: '*Morality is in Europe today herd-animal morality*' and we can thus see how Nietzsche strengthens the

---

[3] In KSA 13, 14[25], written in early 1888, Nietzsche says: "the word classical here used not in the historical sense, but in the psychological one."

emphasis on the value dichotomy. In *On the Genealogy of Morals*, I, 7–8, Nietzsche again sets up a strict dichotomy, this time between 'the aristocratic value-equation (good = noble = powerful = beautiful = happy = beloved of God)' and one which is the reverse of this, associated with the Jews, who made a revaluation of the older values and with whom the slave revolt in morality began. Thus Christianity, Jews, and the slave revolt seem to constitute one side of the dichotomy, and the values before this were Greek and aristocratic, but the nature of the values after a revaluation still remains unspecified.

In *Twilight of the Idols,* we come across the '*first* example of my "revaluation of all values"' (TI 'Errors' 2). Here he 'reverses' the most general formula at the basis of every religion and morality: 'Do this and this, refrain from this and this – and you will be happy! Otherwise . . .'. Nietzsche counters this with the claim that a well-constituted human being, a 'happy one', *must* perform certain actions and instinctively shrinks from other actions. Character, instincts, and will determine actions! This is related to Nietzsche's use of physiology and to his ethics of character or virtue. The drives are prior to virtue and morality. This view has much in common with the older Greek view, which can be exemplified with, for example, Heraclitus: 'Man's character is his fate' and with Greek ethics of virtue. Nietzsche regards ancient morality as essentially a master morality.[4]

In the very last section of *Twilight of the Idols* Nietzsche again gives a specific meaning to the present revaluation of all values:

> Tragedy [. . .] affirmation of life [. . .] is what I called Dionysian [. . .] the eternal joy of becoming [. . .] And with that I again return to the place from which I set out – the *Birth of Tragedy* was my first revaluation of all values: with that I again plant myself in the soil out of which I draw all that I will and *can* – I, the last disciple of the philosopher Dionysus. – I, the teacher of the eternal recurrence . . . (TI 'Ancients' 5)

Note that he claims that tragedy and the Greeks constitute 'the soil out of which I draw all that I will and *can*'. It is difficult for him to be more explicit as to where the foundation of his affirmative values lies. He makes a similar claim in a notebook from 1884: 'The knowledge of the great Greeks has formed me' (KSA 11, 26[3]).[5]

There are three important explicit references to 'revaluation of all values' in *The Antichrist*. The first gives a third description of what this revaluation

---

[4] "This is our difference from the Greeks: their morality grew out of the *ruling* casts." KSA 11, 25[163], early 1884.

[5] "Die Kenntniß der großen Griechen hat mich erzogen: an Heraclit Empedocles Parmenides Anaxagoras Democrit ist mehr zu verehren, sie sind *voller*" [than the great philosophers like Kant, Hegel, Schopenhauer and Spinoza].

means: 'Let us not undervalue this: *we ourselves*, we free spirits, are already a "revaluation of all values"' (A 13). This shows that the revaluation is already occurring and it shows the strong ethics of virtue nature of Nietzsche's thinking, i.e., that the personality is primary and values and actions only secondary. The free spirits are further down in the section associated with realism, scientific method and scepticism. In the penultimate section of *The Antichrist*, we are presented with perhaps the clearest expression of what the revaluation of all values means. Nietzsche here claims that a second revaluation already has been attempted and for a time succeeded, but in the end failed:

> [...] *what* the Renaissance was? The *revaluation of Christian values*, the attempt, undertaken with every expedient, with every instinct, with genius of every kind, to bring about the victory of the opposing values, the *noble* values. ... Up till now *this* has been the only great war, there has been no more decisive questioning than that conducted by the Renaissance – *my* question is its question – : [...] to set the *noble* values on the throne, which is to say to set them *into* the instincts, the deepest needs and desires of him who sits thereon [...] Christianity would thereby have been *abolished*! – What happened? [...] Luther *restored the Church*: he attacked it. ... The Renaissance – an event without meaning, a great *in vain*! – (A 61)

Notice that Nietzsche here, and earlier, refers to '*the* opposing values' (my italics), not a set of opposing values or just opposing values, strongly implying that it is a question of only two alternatives, i.e., a dichotomy of systems of values.

Nietzsche constantly praises the Renaissance highly. Like antiquity, but more rarely and on a lower level, it constitutes an example and model for him. He refers to it as the 'last *great* age' (TI 'Expeditions' 37) and claims that 'in the modern time it is the Italian Renaissance which has brought man the highest' (KSA 10, 7[44]). Both Goethe and Napoleon are associated with the Renaissance (KSA 12, 9[179] and GS 362). He highly commends its sense of *virtù*. Modern man is inferior to the man of the Renaissance but 'the man of the Renaissance, is inferior to the man of antiquity' (KSA 12, 16[111]). The Renaissance is generally regarded as a rebirth of antiquity and was so viewed also by Nietzsche: 'There was [...] in the Renaissance an uncanny and glittering reawakening of the classical ideal, of the noble mode of evaluating all things' (GM I 16). Thus, when he claims that '*my* question is its question' (A 61), he refers to the Renaissance revaluation of Christian values into essentially ancient values.

In the last section of *The Antichrist*, Nietzsche again reaffirms his attack on the present values (so concisely and provocatively expressed in the title of the work itself):

> I *condemn* Christianity [...] The Christian Church [...] has made every value
> a disvalue [...] a conspiracy against health, beauty, well-constitutedness,
> bravery, intellect, *benevolence* of soul, *against life itself* ... [...] And one
> calculates *time* from the *dies nefastus* [unlucky day] on which this fatality
> arose – from the *first* day of Christianity! *Why not rather from its last? – From
> today?* – Revaluation of all values! (A 62)

The last sentence is equivocal but an important sense is surely 'all (Christian)
values have been revalued'. Nietzsche has disclosed Christianity (including
secularized Christianity) and shown us the alternative. We shall not forget that
while writing *The Antichrist* and *Ecce Homo*, he planned three further volumes on
the theme of the revaluation. That last sentence is probably also a (half-hidden)
reference to these three further volumes under the main title of *Revaluation of All
Values*.

Nietzsche's *Ecce Homo* was written after *The Antichrist* but was intended to be
published before it. In the first sentence of the preface, Nietzsche explains the
purpose of the book as a presentation of '*who I am*' – 'I am the disciple of the
philosopher Dionysus' – *before* he will make the heaviest demand on mankind,
that is, the revaluation of all values. The 'revaluation of all values' is the *Leitmotif*
throughout the work and it contains eleven explicit references to it. In the first
two chapters, 'Why I am So Wise' and 'Why I am So Clever', Nietzsche seems to
describe the revaluation as the goal and meaning of his life, and he attempts to
show why he is able to see and do what no one else sees or does.

At the end of his discussion of *The Birth of Tragedy* in *Ecce Homo*, without
using the word revaluation, Nietzsche clearly refers to a revival of Greek values:
'Everything in this essay [*The Birth of Tragedy*] is prophetic: the proximity of
the return of the Greek spirit, the necessity for *counter Alexanders* to *retie* the
Gordian knot of Greek culture after it had been untied ... Listen to the world-
historic accent with which the concept "tragic disposition" is introduced' (EH
'Books' BT:4). With this, Nietzsche also implies that the 'revaluation' is a
theme in his writing from his first book onwards. In the sixth section of his
discussion of *Human, All Too Human* he states that the revaluation is a consequence of historical knowledge, and hence rejects 'utopian' interpretations.
The importance of history for the revaluation, and more concretely, what in
history, is expressed in a note from the first half of 1888: 'I sought in history
the beginning of the construction of reverse ideals (the concepts "pagan",
"classical", "noble" newly discovered and expounded –)' (KSA 13, 16[32]).
In his discussion of *Dawn*, he describes the revaluation as 'an escape from
moral values' which, of course, is fully consistent with his view of himself and
Zarathustra as immoralists. A bit later in the same section, he refers to morality
as the morality of 'unselfing'. Almost always when Nietzsche speaks of

morality, he refers to modern and Christian morality. Thus, even though it does not appear so, the statement 'an escape from all moral values' allows for alternative moral values, for an ancient or master morality. Recall, if you will, Nietzsche's critique of Socrates and Plato for having moralized the world. Nietzsche further in this section describes the positive side of the revaluation: 'in an affirmation of and trust in all that has hitherto been forbidden, despised, accused'. This shows, *pace* the utopian and critical interpretations, that the new values are not unknown, only at present de-valued. This appears to confirm the reversal interpretation, but on closer inspection, it fits the dichotomy interpretation of the revaluation better.

In the first section of Nietzsche's discussion of *Beyond Good and Evil* in *Ecce Homo*, he claims that the affirmative part of his task was already done after having written *Dawn*, *The Gay Science*, and, most importantly, *Thus Spoke Zarathustra* – 'it was the turn of the denying, the No-saying and *No-doing* part: the revaluation of existing values themselves, the great war'. This view of Zarathustra as affirmative and of *Thus Spoke Zarathustra* as an affirmative book is consistent with all Nietzsche's statements about Zarathustra – possessing '*great health*' and as 'this most affirmative of all spirits' – and of his enormous appraisal of the work. What is the nature of the values and the *Weltanschauung* in this work? For Nietzsche *Thus Spoke Zarathustra* is a tragic work.[6] We need to recall that tragedy is for Nietzsche an affirmative art and *Weltanschauung*: 'the *affirmative* pathos *par excellence*, I call the tragic pathos' (EH 'Books' Z:1). When Nietzsche introduces Zarathustra for the first time, in *The Gay Science* 342, this section is called '*Incipit tragoedia*', i.e., 'the tragedy begins', and the section also ends with these words. He uses the same words when he refers to *Thus Spoke Zarathustra* after it was written, in *The Gay Science*, V, 382. From this section he also quotes in *Ecce Homo* at length. In his discussion of *Thus Spoke Zarathustra* in *Ecce Homo*, he refers to it, or aspects of it, five or six times as the concept Dionysus and as being Dionysian, and he refers to the language of Zarathustra as dithyrambic. The *Weltanschauung* is thus, according to Nietzsche, akin to ancient tragedy. We cannot examine all the values expounded in *Thus Spoke Zarathustra* here, but those of 'that decisive chapter' (EH 'Books' Z:1) 'Of Old and New Law-Tables', so suitable for a study of the revaluation of all values, can be commented upon. The theme of this chapter in *Thus Spoke Zarathustra* is clearly one of revaluation even if the expression is not used. About half of the thirty sections of this, the longest chapter in *Thus Spoke Zarathustra*, are critical and give different versions of 'shatter the old law-tables'.

---

[6] For an excellent work on Nietzsche and tragedy, and of *Thus Spoke Zarathustra* as a tragic work, see May (1990: especially Ch. 7). See also Higgins (1987: Ch. 2) and Meyer (2024: Ch. 1).

This critique culminates in the command: 'Shatter, shatter the good and the just!' The new law-tables are only half-written, lying among the old shattered ones. We are given a rather long list – in the form of metaphors and similes – of virtues, descriptions, and imperatives, summarizing most of what has been said earlier in *Thus Spoke Zarathustra*. (Nietzsche did not publish part four of *Thus Spoke Zarathustra* and therefore this section which is placed near the end of part three, can well be seen as a summary.) The affirmative part of this chapter claims that what is good and evil depends on the goal, and the goal is the *Übermensch*. To this theme, a number of concepts are associated: the future, a new nobility, wanting to rule, and life and society as an experiment. We are further given a description of 'the highest soul' and a very large number of 'virtues' are described and recommended: the bestowing virtue, honesty (realism), creativity, courage, dance and laughter, pride and self-love, self-overcoming, and becoming better than the best (compare Nietzsche's interest and praise of the Greek concepts *agon* and *aristeuein*), and willingness to sacrifice oneself and one's neighbours. It culminates in: 'This new law-table do I put over you, O my brothers: *Become hard*!' – for the noble and the creative are hard, and the soft will inevitably adapt themselves to the present values.

The interpretation of *Thus Spoke Zarathustra* as the culmination of Nietzsche's affirmative values is confirmed a little later in *Ecce Homo*, where Nietzsche claims that the domination of Christian values was due to the fact that 'above all, a *counter-ideal* was lacking – until *Zarathustra*' (EH 'Books' GM). Thereafter Nietzsche refers to the tremendous task of the revaluation and speaks of it as a shattering thunderbolt, explaining thereby the title of the last chapter: 'Why I am a Destiny.' In this chapter Nietzsche claims: 'But my truth is *dreadful*: for hitherto the *lie* has been called truth. – *Revaluation of all values*: this is my formula for an act of supreme coming-to-oneself on the part of mankind which in me has become flesh and genius' (EH 'Destiny' 1). Nietzsche here suggests, as he has also done earlier, that the two value systems are not equivalent – not only are they different and of different value, but one is also natural while the other is not. Therefore, the turning, or returning, to the ancient paradigm can be regarded as a 'supreme coming-to-oneself'. Nietzsche continues: 'I contradict as has never been contradicted and am nonetheless the opposite of a negative spirit.' The same statement is repeatedly made about Zarathustra. The reason he can make this apparently paradoxical statement is because he contradicts within one 'paradigm', while praising or pointing at another – or, alternatively, he regards himself as a philosophical physician who is negating a negation, who is attacking a disease and thus, by negating, being curative. Nietzsche continues on this theme in section seven: 'Indeed, this is *my* insight: the teachers, the leaders of humanity, theologians all of them, were also, all of them, decadents: *hence* the revaluation of all values into hostility to life, *hence* morality' (EH 'Destiny' 7).

In section eight, he reconnects to *Thus Spoke Zarathustra* and gives several examples of truths and concepts created by Christian morality but absent among healthy values:

> Have I been understood? I have not just now said a word that I could not have said five years ago through the mouth of Zarathustra – The *unmasking* of Christian morality is an event without equal, a real catastrophe. He who exposes it is a *force majeure*, a destiny [...] The concept 'God' invented as the antithetical concept to life [...] The concept 'soul', 'spirit', finally even 'immortal soul', invented so as to despise the body, so as to make it sick [...] The concept 'sin' invented together with the instrument of torture which goes with it, the concept of 'free will' [...] Finally – it is the most fearful – in the concept of the *good* man common cause made with everything weak, sick, ill-constituted, suffering from itself [...] an ideal made of opposition to the proud and well-constituted, to the affirmative man, to the man certain of the future and guaranteeing the future – the latter is henceforth called the *evil man* ... And all this was believed in *as morality*! – *Ecrasez l'infâme*! (EH 'Destiny' 8)

We can note that according to Nietzsche none of these 'inventions' (with the exception of the immortal soul accepted by, for example, Pythagoras and Empedocles) – the Christian God, sin, free will, and 'goodness' – existed in pre-Socratic Greece. The last section of *Ecce Homo*, essentially Nietzsche's last words, consists of only a few words: 'Have I been understood? – *Dionysus against the Crucified*.'

The first two occurrences of the expression 'revaluation of all values' in Nietzsche's writings can be found in a notebook covering the period of summer and autumn 1884, i.e., about one year before Nietzsche wrote *Beyond Good and Evil* where it first appeared in print (KSA 11, 26[259] and 26[284]).[7] Its very first appearance is as a catchword, as a subtitle to a planned work: '*Philosophy of Eternal Recurrence*: An Attempt at the Revaluation of All Values', that probably represents an early version of Nietzsche's plans for a *Hauptwerk*. The second occurrence is in a note, consisting of three short numbered sections, outlining the planned content of this work. First, the idea of eternal recurrence, its presuppositions, and its consequences are to be introduced. Second, discussion of eternal recurrence as the heaviest thought: and its probable effect if it is not prevented by means of a revaluation of all values. Third, the revaluation of all values is introduced as the means of enduring the idea of eternal recurrence. Pleasure at

---

[7] Thereafter come six occurrences in a notebook that covers a full year, from approximately when Nietzsche started writing *Beyond Good and Evil* until it was published.

uncertainty (rather than certainty), creativity, power, and pride are associated with
the revaluation.

The expression 'revaluation of all values' occurs in two slightly different
senses in Nietzsche's notebooks. In a first sense, it is used mainly as a catchword
in drafts for titles or subtitles (usually for Nietzsche's *Hauptwerk*). The second
sense is more general and similar to how it is used in the published works
already discussed. I have found about two score occurrences, about half of them
as title or subtitle, and half of them as an expression used or discussed.

Of the more general references to revaluation in Nietzsche's notebooks,
several are more or less duplicates of one another, and several are drafts and
very similar to the published statements already discussed. In several of them,
he emphasizes that the old values necessarily lead to pessimism and nihilism.
He emphasizes the strength and importance of the revaluation by claiming that it
will be very costly, a theme discussed in greater detail in *Ecce Homo*, and he
asks questions such as 'How would these men have to be constituted who took
upon themselves this revaluation?' Only four notes will here be used to supplement the previous discussion. All four discuss the revaluation of moral values
and set up slightly different versions of the same dichotomy, that between
a morality of self-denial and one of self-affirmation. In the first of these,
Nietzsche states: 'The ignored main fact: There is a contradiction between
'becoming more moral' and the lifting up and making stronger the type man'
(KSA 12, 2[131]). In the second: 'What has been *deified*? The value instincts in
the community (that which made possible its continued existence). What has
been *slandered*? That which *set apart* the higher men from the lower, the desires
that create clefts' (KSA 13, 16[15]). In the third: 'Not the "moral corruption" of
antiquity, but precisely its *moralization* is the prerequisite through which alone
Christianity could become master of it. Moral fanaticism (in short: Plato)
destroyed paganism, by revaluating its values and poisoning its innocence'
(KSA 13, 16[15]). In the last of these four notes, the dichotomy is made most
explicit:

> The morality of self-denial is the typical morality of decline par excellence
> [...] the teachers, the leaders of mankind were décadents: *therefore* the
> revaluation of all values into the realm of the nihilistic ('the beyond') [...]
> to *liberate* [man] from the morality [...] To *again raise and set up the egoism
> of humankind*! (KSA 13, 23[3], October 1888)[8]

Nietzsche thus wants to see come about, what during the Renaissance most
clearly occurred in the arts: the centre of gravity moved from God, religion,

---

[8] Part of this long note was used in EH "Destiny" 7.

symbolism, and the 'beyond' and instead man and individual men were put in its place.

Nietzsche also uses a large number of synonyms for revaluation. Most frequent are *Umdrehung* and *Umkehrung*, but many others are also used.[9] His use of these is very similar to his use of revaluation and therefore little new information is contained in these expressions for us here. Only one example will be mentioned here. There he claims that really great humans are lacking, and the reason is our herd-animal morality – which 'in Europe today is simply called "morality" – as if there were no other morality and could be no other'. He continues:

> Whoever has thought profoundly about where and how the plant man has hitherto grown most vigorously must conclude that this has happened under the *reverse* conditions [. . .] A morality [must appear] with such reverse intentions, which desires to train men for the heights, not for comfort and mediocrity [. . .] To prepare a *reversal of values* for a certain strong kind of man of the highest spirituality and strength of will [. . .] whosoever reflects on this becomes one of us, the free spirits – to be sure, a different kind of 'free spirit' from those before us; for the latter wanted approximately the opposite of what we do. To us, it seems to me, belong [. . .] all those critics and historians who courageously carry forward the happily-begun discovery of the world of antiquity – it is the work of the *new* Columbuses of the German spirit (for we stand at the beginning of this conquest). For in the world of antiquity there reigned a different, more lordly morality than today; and the man of antiquity, raised in this morality, was a stronger and deeper man than the man of today – he alone has hitherto been 'the man who turned out well'. (KSA 11, 37[8])

Close readings of Nietzsche's late books and his late notes make it possible to identify a rather large number of concrete values that he revalues, such as pity, pride, the 'good man', and the herd animal man.[10]

1.4 The History of the Revaluation Theme in Nietzsche's Thought

There exist two major misconceptions regarding the theme of revaluation of all values in Nietzsche's thought. One concerns its origin (when and in what context did Nietzsche discover the theme) and the other is its meaning (discussed earlier). Almost all literature on the revaluation of all values treats it as having its origin in 1886 or in 1884. To mention just a few examples, Curt Paul Janz, the by far best Nietzsche biographer (whom almost all other biographies

---

[9] Other synonyms or near synonyms are *Umdrehung, Umkehrung, entgegengesetzter Werthe, Werth-Gegensatz, auf den Kopf, transcendence, Umtaufung, entwerthen, Wandel der Werthe,* and *Umsturz.*

[10] I have discussed such concrete revalued values in some of the late books, in my studies Brobjer, 2021, 2023a and 2023b. In a slightly different context, Richardson discusses the revaluing of pity and altruism in *Nietzsche's New Darwinism* (2004: Ch. 5).

are based upon) does not discuss the revaluation of all values before *Beyond Good and Evil* (1886), except briefly in regard to Nietzsche's childhood essay 'Fatum und Geschichte' and regarding a statement in the third *Untimely Meditation*. The valuable entry in the *Nietzsche Handbuch*, written by Andreas Urs Sommer, mentions nothing before 1884, but his immensely rich commentaries *Friedrich Nietzsches 'Der Antichrist': Ein philosophisch-historischer Kommentar* (2000) and *Kommentar zu Nietzsches Der Antichrist, Ecce Homo, Dionysus-Dithyramben und Nietzsche contra Wagner* contain much interesting and relevant material. Philippa Foot, in her 'Nietzsche: The Revaluation of Values', in *Nietzsche: A Collection of Critical Essays*, edited by Robert Solomon (1973), 156–168, refers to no work earlier than *Thus Spoke Zarathustra*. Richard Schacht's *Nietzsche* (1983) contains a long chapter on 'Value and Values', including a long subchapter entitled 'Toward a Revaluation of Values', but only uses and refers to post-*Thus Spoke Zarathustra* books and the notes published as *The Will to Power* (i.e., notes from 1885 to 1888). However, three studies, by Higgins, Ridley, and Owen, seem, without discussion, to place its beginning significantly earlier, in the works *Dawn* (1881) and *The Gay Science* (1882).

The place and development of the revaluation theme in Nietzsche's thought can be summarized as follows.

1880/81	1882	1884	1886	1887/88
Origin of the revaluation theme in notes. Great concern with values.	Important but brief published statement in GS 269.	Becomes a major theme in notes (and a theme in letters). Nietzsche coins the word *Umwertung*.	Becomes an important theme in published BGE. First published use of the word *Umwertung*.	Becomes a major theme in published works and in notes.

To be able to follow the theme of revaluation in Nietzsche's thought it is convenient to go backwards in time. It was Nietzsche who coined the German word '*Umwerthung*', revaluation, and he was thus the first thinker to use the associated expression '*Umwerthung aller Werthe*' and '*Umwerthung der Werthe*' (but he also used a large number of other related synonyms and expressions).[11]

---

[11] *Historisches Wörterbuch der Philosophie*, "Umwertung." However, Andreas Urs Sommer has shown (private communication) that the word Umwertung existed before Nietzsche, in literature

By 1887, in *On the Genealogy of Morals*, and especially by 1888, revaluation had become a major and prominent theme in Nietzsche's thought – and during this time he frequently referred to the theme. It has by now also become not only a *Leitmotif* and *topos*, but also a literary project on which he worked intensively during his final four or five years. This is especially noticeable in *Ecce Homo*, which was written to prepare the ground for his next work, the *Revaluation of All Values* (discussed in Section 2 of this Element).

The first time he used the word 'revaluation' in his published works was in *Beyond Good and Evil* (1886), sections 46 and 203, where he explicitly refers to an earlier revaluation and to the hope for new creative spirits who can 'provide the stimuli for opposite valuations and to revalue and invert "eternal values".' In the former section, he claims that Christianity made a revaluation of ancient values and in the second, he refers to our present need for a new revaluation. Furthermore, revaluation, without reference to that word, is also discussed in many other sections of the book and is a general theme in the book, and he uses many synonyms and alternative expressions for it. From here onwards, it is a major theme in his published writings – but he had developed the topic earlier.

The first time Nietzsche used the word 'revaluation' is in two notes from 1884, where the first is as subtitle to a book project, and the other briefly relates the revaluation to his idea of eternal recurrence. It is in both these cases closely associated with Nietzsche's idea of eternal recurrence. In the first, it is used as a subtitle to a planned but never finished book (which later almost certainly developed into Nietzsche's attempt to write a magnum opus): '*Philosophy of Eternal Recurrence*: An Attempt at the Revaluation of All Values' (KSA 11, 26[259]). The second is a few pages later in the same notebook where he discusses eternal recurrence and what is necessary to live with that thought, and twice answers 'the revaluation of all values', and thereafter gives some examples of such revaluations (joy at uncertainty rather than certainty, belief in creativity rather than in 'cause and effect', no longer will to survival but to power and not to possess defensive but proud subjectivism) (KSA 11, 26[284]).

Shortly before Nietzsche used the word revaluation for the first time, he was much concerned with values and systems of values. Just a few pages earlier in his notebook Nietzsche had read and used his friend Paul Deussen's *Vedanta* and Herman Oldenberg's *Buddha* to create value-dichotomies (with page-references to these works), and he several times used the synonym '*Umkehrung* [. . .] *der Werthschätzungen*', reversal of valuation or esteem, or reversal of the setting of values (KSA 11, 26[221 and 192]). Thus, a contrast with Eastern

---

dealing with economics, but Nietzsche still seems to be the first to have used it in a philosophically relevant sense.

systems of values is likely to have aided and worked as a stimulus for Nietzsche's development of the idea.

Nietzsche had written the third book of *Thus Spoke Zarathustra* in January and February 1884 and read the proofs in March. In the first two books of *Thus Spoke Zarathustra*, the pivotal ideas were the thought of eternal recurrence (although it remained unannounced within the book) and the *Übermensch*. The theme of revaluation is also present, for example, in 'Of the Three Metamorphoses', but perhaps on a more individual rather than social level and not elaborated upon.

We have thus seen that the first time Nietzsche used the word revaluation was in 1884, and more importantly, that he at this time was much concerned with this topic. Should then 1884 be regarded as the year of the birth of the *topos* of the revaluation of all values? Moreover, ought we then to emphasize its close link to the idea of eternal recurrence – which certainly then was an important context?

Maybe, but the *topos* has a distinct prehistory, and it is even expressed in his published writings before then. In section 269 of *The Gay Science* (1882), Nietzsche clearly expresses it: '*In what do you believe? –* In this, that the weights of all things must be determined anew.'[12] This theme resonates strongly in Nietzsche, although its context and its meaning is not elaborated on in the book.

Searching for earlier instances and discussions of the revaluation theme in Nietzsche's notebooks yields interesting and specific results – the theme of revaluation is very present in the notes from 1880/81. I have found over fifty notes in which Nietzsche clearly elaborates on the revaluation theme, but will here only present (in a shortened form) the ten most obvious ones in chronological order:

1. 'Change of valuation.'
2. 'One needs, by means of a radical scepticism in regard to values, first of all to overthrow all value judgments, to have free opportunity.'
3. 'Everything which we now call immoral has somewhere and sometime once been moral. What guarantees that it does not yet again change its name?'
4. 'Christianity made everything interesting again, by turning upside down every value judgment.'
5. '[A] great task has arisen on the horizon before it, namely the revision of every valuation: however, before all things are laid on the scales, the scale itself is necessary – I mean that sort of highest sense of judgment of the highest intelligence.'

---

[12] The revaluation theme is also, but much more vaguely, visible in sections 115, 116, 301, and 335.

6. 'For that *new* values are needed. First a critique and removal of the old.'
7. '*Either* value other things than are valued *or* value things differently than they are valued.'
8. 'For the purpose of changing people: we for once need to assume that *our values* about good and evil acts are *false* and arbitrary, everything needs to be examined anew.'
9. '**Main question: according to what** is the *table of values* determined and changed? So that one property appeared more valuable than another?'
10. '*Change of valuation* – is my task' (KSA 9, 1[56], 3[54, 66, 116, 158], 5[25], 6[175, 378] and 11[20, 76]).

We can note that all of these statements were made before his 'discovery' of eternal recurrence in August 1881, and that Nietzsche's concern with values and the change of values constituted an important context of that discovery. In fact, one can regard the thought of eternal recurrence as the answer to what he asks for and discusses in many of his notes in 1880/81 as the thing that can help one change and evaluate values.

That Nietzsche discovered and developed the theme of revaluation in 1880/81 is also consistent with his own claims in *Ecce Homo*, where he, in his discussion of *Dawn*, with its motto 'There are so many daybreaks that have not yet dawned' writes: 'Where does its author *seek* that new dawn [...]? In a *revaluation of all values*, in an escape from all moral values, in an affirmation of and trust in all that has hitherto been forbidden, despised, accused.' This could have been an example of how Nietzsche reinterpreted his earlier writings in line with his later thought, but the notes from 1880/81 show that this claim was not just a later construction, but was based on, at least in part, views already present at that time. We can also note that there is a dramatic increase in Nietzsche's use of the word 'value' and derivations of that word in 1880/81 (as well as an increase in his use of the word morality and its derivations). We can especially note the increase in his use of the word 'esteem', or setting the value of, 'Werthschätzung' and the word value-judgement, 'Werthurtheil' (which he had never used before 1880). What happened in 1880/81 is that Nietzsche became concerned with values and evaluation in general.[13]

---

[13] It is, of course, possible to go beyond 1880 and find traces of this idea and concern earlier. As any historian will know, it is almost always possible to find earlier traces of anything and any thought. However, these earlier traces are merely traces, not signs of a conscious concern with this concept and idea. Such scattered traces can, for example, be found in Nietzsche's early *Germania* essay "Fate and History" from 1862 and in the third *Untimely Meditation*, *Schopenhauer as Educator*, 3 (1874), and I will discuss a few of them in the chapter "Nietzsche and Ancient Values." What happened in 1880/81 is that the problem of value, morality and change of valuation became a theme or major theme in Nietzsche's thought.

The ten most immediate references to the revaluation theme from 1880/81, quoted earlier, fall into four groups. These seem to correspond well to many of Nietzsche's later and more well-known statements regarding the revaluation of all values.

(i)   Plain statements, with almost no context.
(ii) Critique of Christianity and its values.
(iii) The questioning of old values for the purpose of opening up new perspectives.
(iv) Philosophical examination of values and how to rank them.

There seems to be no one specific context that proves itself much more important than several other ones for the development of the revaluation theme. It is true that the revaluation of all values has a sort of origin in Nietzsche's critique of Christianity, but it is approximately equally true that it has its origin in the context of a more general critique of contemporary values, and in the problems of pessimism (in Nietzsche's important wresting with Schopenhauer), in the contrast expressed by ancient Greek values, and by eastern values, in insight into the errors of old values, and by the simple effect of relativism. Other contexts of these early revaluation-notes include discussions of the devil (and hence evil), increasing critique of anthropocentrism, the debate between egoism and altruism and a general critique of superstition and metaphysics (which many old values are rooted in, according to Nietzsche).

One interesting consequence of dating the origin of the revaluation of all values to 1880/81 is that it affects our view of Nietzsche's overall thought and its development. It is common to divide his thought and writing into three periods: the early (1869–76), the middle (1877–82), and the late (1883–88). There is truth in this view, and Nietzsche himself emphasized both it and the two 'breaks' which it implies. However, in many respects, it is misleading, and a different view is better, as emphasized by Montinari. This second view emphasizes primarily two periods: pre-1880, as the time before Nietzsche fully came into his own (and it can be divided into two further periods, a more idealistic/romantic and a more positivistic one), and one from c. 1880, that of the mature Nietzsche. The difference between these views can be seen as moving the second 'break' from 1882/83 to 1879/80/81 (the time he left his professorship in Basel, began his nomadic period, and made several of his philosophical 'discoveries').[14] When referring to Nietzsche's published books, both pictures can be regarded as approximately equally accurate, but

---

[14] I discuss many of these "discoveries" or themes on pages 82–89, and in the extensive notes, in my book *Nietzsche's Philosophical Context: An Intellectual Biography* (2008).

when it comes to his life, thoughts and notes, the latter is in several respects better since it does not deny the importance of his thought in the early 1880s (such as his severe critique of morality, Christianity and his new concern with values), but instead connects it with his later, post-1882 thought. However, one should be aware that such divisions into two or three periods are constructs, and although they can aid our understanding of Nietzsche's thought, one should use them with care and certainly not as dogma. In important ways, there is, of course, also a continual development throughout Nietzsche's life.[15]

1.5 Values and Revaluation of Values in *Thus Spoke Zarathustra*

Thus Spoke Zarathustra can be regarded as part of Nietzsche's revaluation project, a part that furthermore contains a presentation of a large number of concrete revaluations of values. There are also in the book some principal statements about values and the revaluation of values.

It is possible to argue that the theme of revaluation is equally important in and for *Thus Spoke Zarathustra* as is the idea of eternal recurrence, the *Übermensch* and the death of God (as representing the crisis of values), and all of these themes are also closely related to one another. While Nietzsche worked on *Thus Spoke Zarathustra* in 1883 and early 1884, he wrote extensive notes on values, change of values, the creation of new values and the destruction of old values, but he had not yet coined the word 'revaluation'. There are a large number of alternative expressions and discussions of the revaluation theme in the notes from 1884, so many that it must be regarded as a major and explicit theme at this time.

Surprisingly, the prominence of the theme of value and revaluation of values in *Thus Spoke Zarathustra* has not generally been noted and discussed. In almost all discussions and accounts of *Thus Spoke Zarathustra* three principal themes are listed; eternal recurrence, *Übermensch* and will to power, while the revaluation is ignored or downplayed.

The theme of revaluating values (often in the form of creating new values) is almost as prominent in *Thus Spoke Zarathustra* as the theme of the *Übermensch* (when we simply count how often he uses it), and more so than will to power and eternal recurrence.

Already in the prologue, two goals within the book (and two purposes of the book) are presented and emphasized; the striving for the *Übermensch* and the task of revaluating values: 'Fellow creators the creator seeks, those who inscribe new values on new tablets' (Z I 'Prologue' 9).

---

[15] For a very different periodization of Nietzsche's works, see the discussion in Matthew Meyer's *Reading Nietzsche through the Ancients* (2014: 277f.).

In the very first section of Zarathustra's speeches, 'On the Three Trans-formations', he describes the development of the higher soul, from that of a camel via a lion to a child. These are also the fundamental stages along the road to revaluation – from being diligent and steadfast (holding on to and defending values), to rebelling (negating values) to creating new values (revalu-ation). The creation of new values is emphasized and is that which characterizes the third stage of the transformation, the 'child'. This emphasis on revaluation or creation of new values is then explicitly repeated in two sections in the first book: 'The noble man wants to create what is new and a new virtue' (Z I 'Tree on the Mountainside'), and: 'Around inventors of new values the world revolves' (Z I 'Flies of the Marketplace'). Thereafter it is again strongly emphasized in the last section, 'On the Bestowing Virtue': 'Verily, this is a new good and evil! [. . .] and may the value of all things be posited anew by you! For that you shall be fighters! For that you shall be creators!'

The creation of new values and the revaluation theme is slightly less empha-sized in the second book, but still explicitly present in several sections. In the first, it is referred to by the expression 'and weeds are called wheat', i.e., that it is the wrong values that are praised (Z II 'The Child with the Mirror'). In another, he repeats the claims from book 1, 'Not around the inventors of new noise, but around the inventors of new values does the world revolve; *inaudibly* it revolves' (Z II 'On Great Events'). He also develops the theme further by emphasizing the close connection between creating and destroying: 'And who-ever must be a creator in good and evil: verily, he must first be an annihilator and shatter values. Thus does the highest evil belong to the highest good: but this latter is the creative' (Z II 'On Self-Overcoming').

In the third book the concern with values and new values is again more explicitly present, especially in 'Of Old and New Tablets', the longest section in all of *Thus Spoke Zarathustra*, which seems to summarize much of the contents of the first three books, and in which it becomes the main theme:

> Each one thought he had long since known what was good and evil for man. [. . .] But he it is who creates a goal for mankind and gives the earth its meaning and its future: he it is who *creates* the quality of good and evil in things. [. . .] now he [Zarathustra] sits here and waits, old shattered law-tables around him and also new law-tables – half-written (Z III 'On Old and New Tablets').

The revaluation of values in *Thus Spoke Zarathustra* has only begun; it is only half-done – with old shattered and new half-written law-tables – as a theme at the end of the third part of *Thus Spoke Zarathustra* makes this text almost ideal as a preface or introduction (as 'entrance hall') to the *Umwerthung aller Werthe*, where this work is going to be continued.

The fourth book of *Thus Spoke Zarathustra* (not published by Nietzsche) can be regarded as primarily dealing with an example of a revaluation of the value of '*Mitleid*' (pity or compassion).

Nietzsche emphasizes in *Thus Spoke Zarathustra* that it is the human subject, the I, 'this creating, willing, valuing I, that is the measure and value of things' (Z I 'On Believers in a World Behind'). Later in the text, he defines man as the valuator:

> The human being first put values into things, in order to preserve itself – it created a meaning for things, a human's meaning! Therefore it calls itself 'human' – that is: the evaluator. Evaluating is creating: hear this, you creators! Evaluating is itself the treasure and jewel of all valued things. Through evaluating alone is there value: and without evaluating the kernel of existence would be hollow. Hear this, you creators! Change of values – that means change of creators. Whoever must be a creator always annihilates. (Z I 'On the Thousand Goals and One')

Humans cannot do otherwise than evaluate, and this is good. He continues this theme in *Beyond Good and Evil*, 3.

Closely related to values, as a version of values, is Nietzsche's discussion of virtue, i.e., values related to human character. The fact that he was much more character- and virtue-oriented than concerned with abstract value (this can be reformulated as that Nietzsche had more of an ethics of virtue-oriented morality rather than the more common alternatives in the nineteenth century, deontology and utilitarianism) is reflected in that he refers to virtue much more frequently, twice as often as to value in *Thus Spoke Zarathustra*.[16] He, in agreement with this, speaks more of new conceptions of humans – *Übermenschen* – rather than of new utopias or new abstract ideals.

Nietzsche had been immensely concerned with values ever since 1880. This is reflected in a long note, where he discusses his own intellectual development, written for a preface for a re-publication of *Human, All Too Human* in August–September 1885, where he describes how he transcended metaphysics. He continues:

> But in the background stood a will to a much greater curiosity, yes, to an enormous attempt: the thought dawned on me if it was not possible to reverse all values, and always the same questions came up: what really do all human valuations mean? What do they disclose about the conditions of life, of your life, furthermore of human life, finally of life itself? – (KSA 11, 40[65])[17]

---

16 See Brobjer (2003).

17 Compare also the notes KSA 11, 40[66] and 41[9], also written for a reworking of *Human, All Too Human*.

The four major themes in *Thus Spoke Zarathustra*, the death of God, eternal recurrence, revaluation, and *Übermensch* are closely related and interwoven with one another. Very briefly and simplified: The death of God reflects a crisis of value. This crisis is both further recognized, and ways to heal it are suggested, by the idea of eternal recurrence (which both intensifies our experiences of the crisis and suggests a solution or way towards a solution) and the revaluation of values (which makes a fundamental dichotomy of values apparent and presents more life-affirming values) and the *Übermensch* represents a concrete living solution of a new type of human who is able to live and affirm life and reality without a belief in God and metaphysics.

In Nietzsche's own discussion of *Thus Spoke Zarathustra* in his last book, *Ecce Homo*, it is the two themes of eternal recurrence and revaluation that he emphasizes.

1.6 Nietzsche and Ancient Greek Values

Having established that the values that need to be revalued are those that denigrate reality and life, Christian values and modern values (which are mostly secularized and moralized Christian values), we need to discuss what sort of values they need to be revalued into. There seem to be three main alternatives. Purely personal and individual values, values that are completely new or values that are related to ancient Greek values, that Nietzsche regarded as more life-affirming than modern values. If we understand new values as values that are new to us who live now, all three of these can be combined. The 'new' values need to be personal values, they need to be different from Christian and modern values and they are likely to have close kinship with ancient Greek values (with the values that Nietzsche regarded as the most affirmative of life and reality we know of) – with the values that ruled before the Jewish/Christian/Platonic first revaluation of values.

Already before *The Birth of Tragedy* was published, Nietzsche wrote in his notebooks 'Socrates, the opponent of Dionysus' and 'my philosophy *inverted Platonism*' (KSA 7, 7[101 and 156]). We can here see an early version of Nietzsche's revaluation of all values. In *The Birth of Tragedy*, Nietzsche speaks of Socrates as 'the precursor of an altogether different culture, art and morality' from that of the older Greek one (BT 13). Hence, already in his first work, Nietzsche is aware of the dichotomy of values that later will become one of his main concerns. Another note from 1870/71 seems to reflect Nietzsche's discovery that although modern morality is life-denying, this was not true for that of the Greeks: 'Ethics also as a *mechane* [mechanism, contrivance] of the will to life: not the denial of this will' (KSA 7, 8[78]).

Nietzsche frequently and explicitly made a value-dichotomy between antiquity and modernity, which can be regarded as being closely related to a revaluation, especially in 1875 while working on the never-finished 'Wir Philologen' ('We Classicists'). To select one pregnant example of this tendency: 'My aim is: to create complete hostility between our modern "culture" and the ancient world. Whosoever wants to serve the former must *hate* the latter' (KSA 8, 3[68]).

Nietzsche's revaluation of all values is of course not a simple return to ancient values and even less to ancient society. Nonetheless, a strong case can be made for the radical thesis that ancient Greek values are not only the foundation and starting point of Nietzsche's revaluation but that to a very large extent the revaluation is a revival of ancient values. There are many specific ancient values and attitudes which Nietzsche shared and praised, such as tragedy, virtue as human excellence (*arete*), *eris* (strife), *agon* (competition), realism and naturalistic values. It would be possible to discuss the ancient precursors to all the major *Leitmotifs* in Nietzsche's writings, not just the revaluation.

Almost always when Nietzsche refers to morality, he refers to modern morality (i.e., from Socrates and Plato onwards). He is not alone in using the word morality in this 'restricted' sense – most philosophers and historians have used it in this manner. A consequence of this is that Nietzsche has often been regarded as only criticizing morality – as having or proposing no affirmative values, at least no moral ones. However, this view is not correct. Instead, Nietzsche, especially when morality is understood in its original sense of *ethos*, of being related to character, holds and proclaims moral values which are essentially ancient Greek values (including ethics of virtue), although almost always without referring to them as *moral* values.

However, occasionally he refers to morality in a positive sense. In *Twilight of the Idols,* he refers to 'all naturalism in morality, that is all *healthy* morality' and contrasts it with '*anti-natural* morality, that is virtually every morality that has hitherto been taught, reverenced and preached' (TI 'Morality' 4). In the epilogue to *The Case of Wagner*, Nietzsche claims that noble morality, master morality, affirms life and oneself, and that its opposition to Christian morality is immense. That Greek morality before Socrates for Nietzsche is part of, and the supreme example of, healthy morality can be seen in the few explicit references he makes to it. 'The higher *moral* nature of the Greeks is shown by their wholeness and simplicity' (KSA 8, 6[36]). A common theme in his early writings, that also echoes in his later writings, is the contrast between the older and the later Greek morality: 'The superficiality of all post-Socratic ethics! The profound Hellenic older ethics did not represent itself in form of words and concepts' (KSA 7, 19[60]). Many of his early statements are indirect in the sense that he refers to the superiority of Greek human beings: 'Greeks the *genius* among the peoples [...] The individual raised to his highest powers through the *polis*' (KSA 8, 5[70]) and 'the verdict of the philosophers of ancient Greece on the value of existence says so much more than a modern verdict does because they had life itself before and around them in luxuriant perfection' (*Untimely Meditation* III 3). Nietzsche also refers to Greek culture as a *standard*: 'When the Greek body and the Greek soul "bloomed" [...] there arose that mysterious symbol of the highest world-affirmation and transfiguration of existence that has yet been attained on earth. Here we have a *standard* by which everything that has grown up since is found too short, too poor, too narrow' (KSA 11, 41[7]).[18] That the greatness of the Greeks was according to Nietzsche due, at least partially, to their morality is shown in the following quotation: 'For in the world of antiquity there reigned a different, more lordly morality than today; and the man of antiquity, raised in this morality, was a stronger and deeper man than the man of today – he alone has hitherto been "the man that has turned out well"' (KSA 11, 37[8]). Most explicitly, Nietzsche's view is expressed in a note from 1883: 'I regard Greek morality as the highest so far' (KSA 10, 7[44]).

Greek antiquity also frequently occurs as an example in the writings of the late Nietzsche: 'The highest types hitherto, the Greeks' (KSA 11, 35[47]) and 'the highest type [of ideal]: the classical ideal' (KSA 13, 11[138]). It would be easy to add many more examples.[19]

Occasionally, Nietzsche in line with the revaluation also attempts a valuation of present phenomena, values, and thought in terms of antiquity or by asking what would the ancients have thought of it: 'The *ancient world* has in fact always been understood only *in terms of the present* – and will *the present* now be understood *in terms of the ancient world*?' (KSA 8, 3[62]) and 'I do not doubt that the first thing an ancient Greek would remark in us Europeans of today would also be self-diminution – through that alone we should be "contrary to his taste"' (BGE 267).

Nietzsche's constant high praise of the Renaissance, including calling it an attempted revaluation, can and ought also to be regarded as relating to a revival of antiquity, and to healthier values.

---

[18] This whole note is pertinent. In it, Nietzsche claims that "Dionysus is a judge" in the sense that antiquity is the judge of modernity.

[19] A few other examples of late references to Greece as an example and ideal are: "The best turned out, most beautiful, most envied type of humanity to date, those most apt to seduce us to life, the Greeks" (BT "ASC" 1). "Oh, those Greeks! They knew how to live!" (GS "Pref" 4). "The whole labour of the ancient world *in vain*: I have no word to express my feelings at something so dreadful" (A 59). "Den Menschen über sich hinaus steigern, gleich den Griechen" (KSA 10, 9[29]). "Heimisch sein in der griechischen Welt!" (KSA 11, 41[4]).

In the last section of the first essay of *On the Genealogy of Morals* (GM I 17), Nietzsche speaks of 'that greatest of all conflicts of ideals' and then rhetorically asks, 'Must the ancient fire not some day flare up much more terribly, after much longer preparation? More: must one not desire it with all one's might? even will it? even promote it?'

1.7 The Relation between the Revaluation and the Idea of Eternal Recurrence

As we have seen earlier, in Section 1.3, the first time Nietzsche uses and coins the expression 'eternal recurrence', in August 1881, KSA 9, 11[141], was at the time when he had worked intensively with value, values and valuation for some time. The first time he used and coined the word '*Umwerthung*', 'revaluation', after having been much concerned with values, how to evaluate them and with new values for several years, in the summer of 1884, he actually uses it in a title of a work which was meant to deal with both eternal recurrence and the revaluation of all values: '*Philosophy of Eternal Recurrence*: An Attempt at Revaluation of All Values' (KSA 11, 26[259]). This work was almost certainly closely related to, or identical with, the work called *Midday and Eternity*, that he soon would refer to as his *Hauptwerk*. The second time he uses the expression 'revaluation of all values' is again related to the idea of eternal recurrence; the revaluation as a condition to endure this idea (KSA 11, 26[284]). It is clear that Nietzsche saw a very close relation between eternal recurrence and revaluation of all values. We would not endure the thought of having to re-live our lives in identically the same way an infinite number of times with our present values – with our Christian and modern values – the thought of eternal recurrence requires us to revalue values.

These two ideas – themes or philosophemes – constitute the central ideas of his work on the *Hauptwerk*, as we will discuss in Section 2. The importance of revaluation can be seen by how often he, already from early on, uses it for a large number of his drafts of titles of his *Hauptwerk*. In fact, the fourth time he uses the expression 'revaluation' at all is again, like the first time, for a title of that work, now from the summer of 1886 in Sils-Maria: '*The Will to Power: Attempt at a Revaluation of All Values*. In four books', with a brief description of the four books. Book one about nihilism – '*as the necessary consequence of the present valuations*'. Book two about a critique of values. Book three about how humans must be constituted to value in a reverse way. Book 4 (called 'the hammer') about the idea of eternal recurrence (KSA 12, 2[100]).

The fifth time he uses the expression 'revaluation' is shortly thereafter in a four-page-long important note in which he continues to elaborate on the contents of the *Hauptwerk*, in line with the previous note, but now with much more detail (KSA 12, 2[131]). Also, the sixth time he uses it is again in a draft of a title of the *Hauptwerk*, in four volumes (KSA 12, 5[75]). In the autumn of 1888, he several times used both these expressions, revaluation and eternal recurrence, in his draft for the *Hauptwerk*, both under the title *Will to Power* and *Umwerthung aller Werthe* (KSA 13, 18[17], 19[8] and 22[14]).

We can thus see that the first ten times he uses the term 'revaluation' he almost always does so together with the expression 'eternal recurrence', and in relation to his *Hauptwerk*.

How are we to understand this close relation between the idea of eternal recurrence and the revaluation of all values? Normally they are by scholars and commentators discussed and elaborated on individually and separately, but Nietzsche connects them. I believe that especially the idea of eternal recurrence is easier to understand when treated together with the revaluation of all values.

Already in the first note where Nietzsche discusses the idea of eternal recurrence, he emphasizes that its effect is the 'eternal importance' of our knowledge, errors, our habits, our lives (he will soon add our values). 'Now comes the most difficult knowledge [eternal recurrence] and makes all sorts of life dreadfully serious.' Imagine the whole of history eternally repeated, he writes: 'Not to be thrown over by that thought, our sense of compassion must not be great.' But taking on ourselves all of past and future suffering is too much for us, Nietzsche argues in this early note, 'but whether *we* still *want to live* is the question, and how!' (KSA 9, 11[141]). Immediately thereafter Nietzsche writes in another note: 'If you fully accept the thought of thoughts [i.e. the idea of eternal recurrence] it will transform you. For everything you want to do, the question becomes: "Is it so that I want to do it infinitely many times?" this is the *greatest* weight' (KSA 9, 11[143]). Shortly thereafter he writes: 'Let us press the image of eternity on *our* life! This thought contains more than all religions, which teaches this life as a brief contempt and to look for an undetermined *other* life' (KSA 9, 11[159]). Soon Nietzsche argues that to live with this thought, to affirm *this* life, we need to get rid of sin and morality – and to revalue our values.

The main point of Nietzsche's thought of eternal recurrence is not a physical theory about that everything is repeated, but a thought experiment or hypothesis that forces us to take and experience life as thousandfold more important than before. This leads us to want to *value* life so that we want to live again. For that, we need to take away, revalue, things that reduce our valuation of life and our desire to live again. Most obviously this means for Nietzsche sin, morality and Christianity (which makes us seek meaning and value *beyond* life), but equally obvious, pessimism (which precisely says that life is not worth living) and nihilism (which says that nothing matters, nothing has any value).

2 *Revaluation of All Values* as a Four-Volume Literary Project

2.1 Introduction to Section 2: *Revaluation of All Values* as Nietzsche's Magnum Opus

There can be no doubt that Nietzsche planned to write a philosophical magnum opus during a period of many years, almost always in four volumes. He explicitly states this a very large number of times in his letters, in his notes and in his published books (including on the back cover of *Beyond Good and Evil*), and there are a very large number of notes related to this project among Nietzsche's papers, including many draft tables of contents for the four volumes. Nietzsche spent much more time and effort on this project than on any of his published books and regarded it as much more important. It has been a major failure of most of Nietzsche research, and even more of the many biographers of Nietzsche, that it and they have not examined and discussed this more.

The possible controversy about the magnum opus concerns if, and then when, Nietzsche perhaps gave up on this project. The standard view is that Nietzsche gave up on it at the end of November 1888, just a little more than a month before his mental collapse. This view is almost certainly wrong and contains two major problems.

(i) Nietzsche never stated that he gave up on the project (since he did not). That he (possibly) did so is a (faulty) conclusion of modern scholars based merely on that Nietzsche after about 20 November 1888 referred to *The Antichrist* in a few letters as 'the *Revaluation of All Values*' rather than as 'the first book of the *Revaluation of All Values*'. This does not necessarily mean that he had given up on the project. On the contrary, there can be several reasons for this and I will show that he had referred to *The Antichrist* as the *Revaluation* already earlier (when there can be no doubt that he regarded it as part of his four-volume magnum opus), and, more importantly, quote two occasions where he as late as in middle of December 1888, just weeks before his mental collapse, still refers to *The Antichrist* as 'the first book of the *Revaluation of All Values*'.

(ii) Even if Nietzsche had given up on the project at the end of November 1888, almost certainly as a consequence of his impending mental collapse, this changes almost nothing. First, it still means that he planned and worked hard to write a four-volume magnum opus for about five years or more, including while writing his late books, from *Thus Spoke Zarathustra* onwards. If he changed his mind after having written *Twilight of the Idols, The Antichrist* and *Ecce Homo* in 1888, it is merely of biographical interest. Second, he did no philosophical work after late November 1888; at least we have no serious philosophical notes from this time or later. The work on a philosophical magnum opus remains Nietzsche's by far largest and most prolonged philosophical project!

For those who are interested in Nietzsche's thought and philosophy, this is his most important and relevant project – far more so than any of his published books. It has one major drawback for us. Of the four planned volumes, three remain uncompleted or unfinished. This is a disadvantage, but not only so. It seems to me that it is quite suitable for a thinker of such dynamic philosophy as Nietzsche's that what we have is not merely a static set of finished positions, but rather ample material for developing many of his most interesting thoughts, including the revaluation of all values.

I will in this second part of this study show that we possess many hundreds of pages of interesting and detailed notes and tables of contents for how Nietzsche planned to develop his thought. We are not only left with *The Antichrist* and three further unwritten volumes about which we know little or nothing. We possess much information about the planned contents of the three unfinished volumes, and there are things to learn from the first volume, *The Antichrist*, about the planned further three volumes. Nietzsche even, immediately after having finished *The Antichrist*, began working and drafting large sections of volume 3, *The Immoralist*, notes that seem not even to have been translated into English until very recently. These notes cover approximately ten pages that he worked on until or near 15 October 1888 (KSA 13, 23[3–7]). Thereafter Nietzsche's notebooks only contain another thirty-three pages in the KSA version. Most of these are filled with notes for *Ecce Homo*, a few late additions for *Twilight of the Idols* and some general notes on other topics.

A great part of Nietzsche's notes for the *Hauptwerk* is from, or were revised in, 1887 and 1888, and thus represents Nietzsche's last evolving philosophical views. Furthermore, among these are detailed plans of the contents of the four planned volumes, plans that Nietzsche used when drafting the contents of volume 1 during the spring of 1888, then dealing with truth and nihilism. When he decided in September 1888 that volume 1 instead was to deal with a critique of Christianity, and the previous volume 1 then became volume 2, he again used these plans and notes to draft the contents of *The Antichrist*. Nietzsche had a remarkably consistent view about the contents of the planned *Hauptwerk*. The last three volumes of the magnum opus remain unwritten, but we have much information about what Nietzsche planned to write in them. We ought to study, discuss, and use this.

The fact that Nietzsche planned and worked extensively on a magnum opus has major consequences both for what is included and what he left out of the books he published in his last years. It also has consequences for how we regard and treat Nietzsche's notes (*Nachlass*).

2.2 The Debate and Controversy about the Planned Magnum Opus

2.2.1 The Status of Nietzsche's Notes

The most common attitude towards Nietzsche's late notes today is that they represent discarded material,[20] and that they, when not overlapping with what is said in his published books, should not be taken as Nietzsche's view. We see a similar view in Hollingdale:

> The *Nachlass* can be read with profit only by someone familiar with Nietzsche's published works, the reason being the above-mentioned fact that its content is rejected material [*sic*] [...] the only principle which does not impose a spurious order upon it is that of comparison and collation with the published work. It falls into two large divisions: (i) preliminary drafts or parallel formulations of something already published, and therefore rejected as superfluous; and (ii) material set aside as being for one reason or another unacceptable. [...] in the latter [case] one must [...] exclude the aphorism from any formulation of Nietzsche's philosophy, since this is precisely what Nietzsche himself did. And one must be capable, of course, of distinguishing between the former kind of material and the latter. The basic consideration to be kept in mind all the time is that anything in the *Nachlass* which cannot be paralleled in the published works is *not valid*.[21]

Alan Schrift (2011) summarizes the position as follows.

> the *Nachlass* does present a great deal of philosophical material that never makes its way into the published texts. [...] The status of this material has been controversial: should it be used to support interpretations of Nietzsche's published works? Should its failure to appear in the published works be taken as evidence that Nietzsche definitively rejected the ideas? In many cases, especially in the late *Nachlass*, it is simply impossible to tell whether an idea was set aside as unworthy or simply never returned to because of Nietzsche's collapse. For the Nietzsche scholar, this is, I believe, a reason to be extremely cautious in terms of presenting the ideas in the *Nachlass* as *Nietzsche's* ideas. (Had he written something and later added: 'but this is wrong!', we would

---

[20] See Magnus (1988: 161), who refers to Nietzsche's notes as "dustbin manuscripts" (and in the connecting footnote 23, Nietzsche's notes are dismissed as "discarded" material). See also Magnus (1986).

[21] Hollingdale (1999: 223).

have a different case, but he rarely does this.) Several years ago, Bernd Magnus drew a distinction between two approaches to Nietzsche's *Nachlass,* dividing Nietzsche's principal commentators into 'lumpers' (including Heidegger, Jaspers, Danto, Schacht, Deleuze, and Müller-Lauter), for whom the status of the *Nachlass* is unproblematic, thus treating it as on at least a par with Nietzsche's published writings; and 'splitters' (including Alderman, Hollingdale, Strong, Montinari, and himself), who 'distinguish sharply between published and unpublished writings'. Since Magnus first drew this distinction, and since the Colli-Montinari edition has become the canonical edition, the number of scholars who simply lump all of Nietzsche's writings together, treating published and unpublished works in the same way, has dwindled to near zero, especially in the English-speaking Nietzsche scholarly community.

This is claimed without any motivation, and without showing that this is the case, for example by showing that much of what can be found in Nietzsche's *Nachlass* is rejected material. Nietzsche, in fact, often did strike out many notes, unlike what Schrift implies. He struck out about 10 per cent of the notes in the three notebooks W II 1–3, used in 1887 and 1888, visible in KGW IX, but not mentioned in KSA or the standard KGW (I-VIII). He seems to have done this mostly because either he had used them for writing *The Case of Wagner,* *Twilight of the Idols* or *The Antichrist,* or because he had copied them over into other later notebooks.

However, oddly enough, Magnus, Hollingdale, Schrift, et al. ignore that Nietzsche, in the last active five years of his life, had great plans and collected many notes to be used for his *Hauptwerk,* but then suddenly collapsed on 3 January 1889. These notes, the majority of which are from the last years, were obviously not discarded and do not fall into the unfortunate dichotomy between either published notes (and variants of this) or discarded notes (which actually seem to be very few). They instead fall into a third category of notes Nietzsche wrote, collected, organized, and revised for use in his planned four-volume *Hauptwerk.*

Jing Huang has recently written an excellent paper on how Nietzsche's notes have been viewed in the Anglo-Saxon world, summarizing much of the debate. She correctly points out that 'We should not forget that Nietzsche's work was interrupted forever in one of the most productive periods of his life', and summarizes the fact that Nietzsche wanted some of his notes, a small amount, burnt in 1888, which 'neither suggests the abandonment of the project of the will to power [the *Hauptwerk*], nor warrants a devaluation of the *Nachlass*'.[22]

---

[22] Huang (2019: 1206 and 1196).

2.2.2 The Debate about Nietzsche's Planned Magnum Opus

The best, the most authoritative, and the most influential text written about Nietzsche's notes and his plans for a *Hauptwerk* since the Second World War is Mazzino Montinari's excellent essay 'Nietzsches Nachlaß von 1885 bis 1888 oder Textkritik und Wille zur Macht' published in *Nietzsche lesen* (1982).[23] As a very acute and perceptive scholar, and as the editor of the critical edition of Nietzsche's works, his views and arguments must certainly be taken very seriously. He is very sceptical, critical, and even hostile towards the idea of a *Hauptwerk* by Nietzsche, and he claims that '*Nietzsche's collapse in Turin came when he literally was finished with everything*' (Montinari 1982: 102). The same claim is made by the main biographer Curt Paul Janz: 'with it [*Der Antichrist*] and by 30 September 1888 his philosophy has come to an end!' (Janz 1993 III: 20f.). To me, this claim seems both psychologically improbable and in regard to what Nietzsche writes simply wrong. The claim that Nietzsche was 'finished with everything' is problematic and misleading. Primarily, it is problematic because it lets Nietzsche's purported intention during the last few weeks of his active life (in spite of his mental state, including severe megalomania) annul his clearly expressed intention for and work on a *Hauptwerk* the previous five years. It is based on two related premises: a letter from 11 December 1888 in which Nietzsche claims '*everything is finished*', and other letters from late November 1888 in which he possibly seems to refer to *The Antichrist* as his complete *Hauptwerk* (KSB 8:1187 and 1159).

It is not clear what Nietzsche refers to when he says that '*everything is finished*' in a letter to Carl Fuchs – it is possible or probable that he is just referring to the work at hand, the first volume of his *Hauptwerk*, as well as the two preparatory texts *Twilight of the Idols* and *Ecce Homo*.[24]

---

[23] This essay has also been published, in slightly different forms, in several other publications, including in the commentary volume to Nietzsche's works, KSA 14, as well as translated into English in *Reading Nietzsche* (2003), 80–102.

[24] The difficulty to know exactly what Nietzsche meant is made more difficult by the fact that this is stated at the very beginning of the letter, which is likely to be a response to a letter by Fuchs that is no longer extant, so that we lack a context to the claim, or to Nietzsche's previous letter (that probably is lost). If Fuchs in his letter discussed *The Antichrist* and/or Nietzsche's life (*Ecce Homo*) and/or critique of Christianity, Nietzsche's statement would seem to refer to these works. In his last pervious extant letter to Fuchs, 9 September 1888 (KSB 8:1104), Nietzsche speaks about *Twilight of the Idols*, *The Case of Wagner* and then adds: "the next that *then* comes is the *Revaluation of All Values* (which first book is almost finished)." When Nietzsche later in the letter from 11 December (KSB 8:1187) says that one can now say things about him that two years later will seem like silliness, it seems possibly to refer to the further three volumes of the *Hauptwerk* that will need time to be written and published. Furthermore, Nietzsche's statement can be influenced by his request that Fuchs should write something

The second part, that Nietzsche gave up the idea of publishing a four-volume *Hauptwerk*, is based on the fact that Nietzsche refers to *The Antichrist* as the *Umwerthung aller Werthe*, and no longer only as the first volume of the *Umwerthung* in two letters from late November 1888. Furthermore, he sometime in December wrote a new title page with the subtitle, instead of the original 'the First Book of the *Revaluation of All Values*' with only '*Revaluation of All Values*'. However, he kept the original title page so there are thus two slightly different title pages in the printer's manuscript copy, so it is not certain that he changed his mind. The changed subtitle may not necessarily reflect a change in the number of volumes, but merely that each of them could be read in any order, and independently of the others (and all four could then have the latter subtitle, *Revaluation of All Values*), which is consistent with how *The Antichrist* is written. The standard interpretation is thus mainly based on a few of Nietzsche's letters, the earliest to Brandes, 20 November and to Deussen, 26 November 1888 (KSB 8:1151 and 1159). It is not altogether unlikely that what Nietzsche referred to in these letters was his present work, and that he simply decided not to speak of the three remaining forthcoming volumes. Nietzsche had, in fact, in letters already before mid-November seemingly referred to *The Antichrist* as the complete *Umwerthung aller Werthe* in that manner, by not referring to it as the first volume, though, clearly, he regarded it as only the first volume at that time. Furthermore, the fact that Nietzsche twice thereafter, in the second half of December, refers to *The Antichrist* as the first book of the *Revaluation* seems to nullify Montinari's and the standard interpretation, as well as that interpretation of the letter to Fuchs.

Montinari's interpretation of this, that Nietzsche had decided not to go on and write the remaining three books of the planned *Hauptwerk*, seems perhaps possible, but it is not the only interpretation. Against this stands the fact that Nietzsche referred to *The Antichrist* as the first book of the *Revaluation* in several letters as late as in mid-November 1888 (to Overbeck and Meta von Salis, 13 and 14 November 1888, KSB 8:1143 and 1144), after which there are no philosophical notes and work. Nietzsche had for over five years been planning and working on a four-volume work, and he had also promised in print, as we will see, in most of his late books to publish such a work. There is nothing in Nietzsche's few notes or in his many letters from mid-November that seems to reflect such a major change in his thought as giving up these plans would be. Furthermore, in the proofs for the *Ecce Homo* manuscript

---

about him (and then it is obviously better if things are finished), and the letter is obviously influenced by Nietzsche's impending collapse.

(as well as in an unused note for *Nietzsche contra Wagner*), *The Antichrist* is referred to as 'the first book of the *Revaluation of All Values*' in the second half of December (as I will show). We also know that after he had finished *The Antichrist*, he set to work on *The Immoralist*, and worked on that until he in mid-October decided that he needed to write *Ecce Homo* as preparatory to the *Revaluation*.

Alan Schrift, in 'Nietzsche's Nachlass' (quoted earlier), while discussing Nietzsche's plans for a *Hauptwerk*, follows Montinari in every detail.

Julian Young, in his *Friedrich Nietzsche: A Philosophical Biography* (2010), does not really discuss Nietzsche's plans and work on a *Hauptwerk* during five years. However, he has a separate chapter dealing with Nietzsche's plans for a *Hauptwerk*, placed after he had finished dealing with Nietzsche's active life, including 1888, chapter 26: 'The Rise and Fall of "The Will to Power".' He limits his discussions exclusively to the plans for the *Hauptwerk* while it was entitled *Der Wille zur Macht*, that is from August 1885 to August 1888, and closely associates it with Nietzsche's philosopheme will to power. He argues that Nietzsche gave up on this theme (although Nietzsche actually continues to refer to it also in *Ecce Homo*), and therefore also on the *Hauptwerk*. Young thereby fails to see the larger picture and ends up discussing a pseudo-problem, why *Der Wille zur Macht* was never completed rather than why the planned magnum opus was never completed and why it was renamed (534). Nonetheless, Young admits that 'the *Revaluation* [can be seen] as a continuation of the 'masterwork' project' (541), but argues like Montinari, without referring to him, that the two letters from the end of November show that it 'in the end abbreviated itself into *The Antichrist*' (542). He does not refer to Nietzsche's later references to *The Antichrist* as the first book of the *Hauptwerk*, nor to the degree that the decision was influenced or determined by Nietzsche's mental state. However, he does, I believe correctly, reject Nietzsche's very late change of the subtitle of *The Antichrist* to *Curse on Christianity*, because 'Nietzsche was almost certainly insane when he created it' (542).

However, to repeat, the second problem with Montinari's interpretation (if it was to be correct) is that it accepts the collapsing of Nietzsche's statements as annulling his earlier view, which is much more relevant, for that was when he worked as a philosopher, from 1884 to late in 1888, from *Thus Spoke Zarathustra* to *Ecce Homo*. The Montinari interpretation uses a few statements from when Nietzsche was mentally unstable to interpret backwards. Throughout Nietzsche's late period, he intended and worked on a *Hauptwerk*, which was never completed, but nonetheless affected the contents of all of his late books and late notes. Even if Nietzsche changed his mind, during the end of November or December 1888, just weeks before his total collapse (at a time when he no longer wrote any philosophical notes, and his judgement was clearly affected by the impending collapse) it does not change that while he was healthy and wrote his late books and notes he planned to write a four-volume *Hauptwerk*. At a minimum, one needs to be aware of this when discussing these books and these notes. Actually, there are good grounds to assume that there is much interesting material in Nietzsche's late notes that is not present or developed in his published books, since he saved it for the *Hauptwerk*. There is much material that awaits closer examination and discussion in the future.

2.3 The History of Nietzsche's Planned Magnum Opus

It seems psychologically unlikely that Nietzsche was finished with everything when he collapsed forty-four years old. The evidence seems also to show that this was not the case. For many years, he had planned and worked hard to write a major work beyond what we have today, and at least as late as November 1888, he still planned to write and publish the three remaining volumes of his *Hauptwerk*. Even if he perhaps gave up the idea of writing a *Hauptwerk* during the last weeks before the mental collapse (and it seems in that case reasonable to regard this, in large part, as due to his mental state), it seems more interesting and relevant to take into consideration his intention and work during the last five years when he wrote all the books of the late phase and when most of his life was directed towards writing the *Hauptwerk*.

The Nietzsche scholar and editor Mazzino Montinari, and almost all commentators thereafter, have regarding the question concerning Nietzsche's magnum opus 'interpreted backwards', that is, from the fact that no *Hauptwerk* was finished (for few accept *The Antichrist* as such), and possibly strengthened by the interpretation that Nietzsche perhaps gave up the idea of a *Hauptwerk* during the last weeks of his active life, they have concluded that Nietzsche's final position was that he had said all he wanted to say. This view became even more entrenched due to the exposure of the problematic nature of Elisabeth's and Peter Gast's selection of notes under the title *Der Wille zur Macht* (1901, 1906), which by many was wrongly understood to constitute this planned *Hauptwerk*. In the debate about its status, the claim that Nietzsche at the end had no intention to write such a work was an effective argument.

It is surprising that Elisabeth's and Peter Gast's *Der Wille zur Macht* has received so much attention and that it is essentially the only attempt at constructing – or seriously discussing – the content of Nietzsche's planned *Hauptwerk*. There ought to be ample room for discussion, speculation, and for producing interesting editorial versions of his notebooks, and thus for examining the relation between the late notes and the published works.[25] The only exception seems to be Friedrich Würzbach's attempt *Umwertung aller Werte: Aus dem Nachlass zusammengestellt und herausgegeben* (München, second ed. 1969). In fact, both of these versions are more like subjective selections from Nietzsche's notes and attempts at organizing them (and thus really not all that different from the many shorter and more random selections from the late Nietzsche's notebooks that have been published) rather than attempts to follow Nietzsche's own intentions. It is, in fact, at least in outline, possible to follow Nietzsche's intentions, but this has not been done.

Still more surprising, considering that it coloured and partly determined much of Nietzsche's life and work during the last five years of his active life, is that the question of his attempt to write a *Hauptwerk* has received almost no in-depth discussion in the many biographies of Nietzsche. It is, for example, only briefly discussed by Janz, and hardly mentioned at all in most other ones, by, e.g., Rüdiger Safranski, *Nietzsche: Biographie seines Denkens* (2000), Josef Rattner, *Nietzsche: Leben – Werk – Wirkung* (2000), Curtis Cate, *Friedrich Nietzsche* (2002), Julian Young, *Friedrich Nietzsche: A Philosophical Biography* (2010), and Sue Prideaux, *I Am Dynamite* (2018).

Essentially, all discussions of the question of whether Nietzsche intended to write a magnum opus, or of the relevance of his late notebooks, have exclusively focused on the project 'Der Wille zur Macht', and inevitably got bogged down in discussions of Elisabeth's and Peter Gast's selection of notes. That has been a serious mistake, for Nietzsche's intention to write a *Hauptwerk* influenced and shaped what he published (and did not publish) during his whole late period.

Many readers of Nietzsche find it surprising and frustrating that he himself claims that the idea of eternal recurrence is so profound and fundamental, but that he hardly elaborates on it at all. In fact, his most comprehensive published 'discussion' of it is in its very first presentation in *The Gay Science* and more poetically in *Thus Spoke Zarathustra*. Thereafter he frequently alludes to it – see, for example, the last sentence of *Twilight of the Idols* – but he does not carry out any discussion of it or its consequences. *There was, however, a reason for this, and that was that he saved it to constitute the pinnacle of his Hauptwerk*, as is shown in almost all of his drafts. The same frustrated expectation can be held about several other aspects or topics of Nietzsche's late thought, especially regarding the revaluation of all values and nihilism. In fact, for the latter case, Nietzsche has even at the end of *On the Genealogy of Morals* promised that

---

[25] There is not even an entry for discussions of Nietzsche's planned *Hauptwerk* in the most extensive of Nietzsche bibliographies, the *Weimarer Nietzsche-Bibliographie*.

he would elaborate more extensively on 'the history of European nihilism' in his *Hauptwerk* (and there are ample notes on this theme among his late notebooks).[26] To deny that Nietzsche had such intentions, and to ignore the late Nietzsche's many interesting notes, has been a failure and a sign of poverty in Nietzsche research over the last decades, in fact, ever since Montinari's critical edition (KSA and KGW) made such studies feasible. Now, when the facsimile and diplomatic edition of Nietzsche's late notebooks have been published as KGW IX in fourteen volumes (2001–23), such an approach can be performed under better conditions than ever before. A thorough examination and study of the late notes, and a comparison of them with his published works, ought to be one of the major tasks of Nietzsche's research today.

Did Nietzsche intend and plan to write a magnum opus, a *Hauptwerk*? I will show that this was indeed the case, that he for at least the last five years of his active life, 1884–88, planned, projected, and worked hard to write such a work. Actually, the project seems to have begun much earlier, already in 1881, but from this time we have much less relevant notes extant. This plan and intention were part of the reason that he felt that he was moving into a new third phase of his development in 1881/82. Nietzsche's plans for and work on his *Hauptwerk* have consequences that we ought to take into consideration. For example, an awareness that he avoided to use the material intended for the *Hauptwerk* when writing *Beyond Good and Evil* and *On the Genealogy of Morals*, and that the subtitle to the former work, '*Prelude to a Philosophy of the Future*' actually refers to that it should be regarded as a prelude to the projected four-volume *Hauptwerk* (which was also listed as a work in progress on the back cover). Further, a consequence of an awareness that Nietzsche worked intensively on writing a magnum opus the last five years of his life, is that the relevance and importance of some topics – such as eternal recurrence, nihilism, values and evaluation – that are present in the late Nietzsche's published books, but which he intended to elaborate on much more in his magnum opus, ought to be given more attention and greater weight. This then also becomes true of his late notes generally. His work on a *Hauptwerk* shows that the late Nietzsche had intentions, and a sense of mission, that went beyond what can be found in the published works since he never finished the said *Hauptwerk*. Not only *Beyond Good and Evil*, but also *On the Genealogy of Morals*, *Twilight of the Idols* and *Ecce Homo*, he regarded, and stated in letters, as preludes to that planned *Hauptwerk*. Furthermore, Nietzsche was hardly a systematic philosopher, but he intended to write this *Hauptwerk* in a more

---

[26] My argument is not so much that Nietzsche had an exoteric and an esoteric philosophy – but that he alluded to things that he was going to make public, but in the end did not due to his mental collapse.

systematic manner than most Nietzsche scholars assume or are aware of, as he stated, and as we can see by the first and only finished volume, *The Antichrist*. I will show herein that we are able to know fairly much about the intended content of the *Hauptwerk*.

At least from 1884, he stated in several letters that *Thus Spoke Zarathustra* only represented a 'Vorhalle' or 'entrance hall' to his philosophy, the 'main building' he planned to work through in the next years. From 1886, he began to explicitly refer to that projected work as a *Hauptwerk*. The evidence for this intention to write a *Hauptwerk* can be seen in his published works, in his letters and in his notebooks. Let us examine the evidence in more detail.

The intention of writing a *Hauptwerk* is visible in all of Nietzsche's books after *Thus Spoke Zarathustra* (and perhaps also in *Zarathustra*, with its inconclusive ending), but this presence has been ignored or gone unnoticed by almost all commentators. He avoided using the material intended for the *Hauptwerk* when he wrote and put together his first book after *Thus Spoke Zarathustra*, *Beyond Good and Evil* (1886) and also *On the Genealogy of Morals* (1887), as stated by Montinari (KSA 14, 346). As we have seen, the subtitle of *Beyond Good and Evil* refers to the *Hauptwerk*, and it was also announced as a work in progress on the back cover. At the end of *On the Genealogy of Morals* he explicitly refers to his future intention: 'I shall probe these things more thoroughly and severely in another connection (under the title "On the History of European Nihilism"; it will be contained in a work in progress: *The Will to Power: Attempt at a Revaluation of All Values*)' (GM III 27).[27] Shortly after having finished writing the three essays of *On the Genealogy of Morals*, he writes to Gast, on 15 September 1887, that he has more to say than what is written in them, with obvious reference to his forthcoming *Hauptwerk*. He planned a second volume of *On the Genealogy of Morals*, with at least three further essays, that later was merged with the plans for the third volume of the *Hauptwerk*, *The Immoralist*. After having finished *On the Genealogy of Morals*, Nietzsche intended to work more or less exclusively on his *Hauptwerk* for a longer period of time – and this was largely what happened. However, he made two short 'pauses' to write *The Case of Wagner* and *Twilight of the Idols* during the following year, both of which he regarded as resting places in the midst of the greater and much more difficult task of writing his *Hauptwerk*. In *The Case of Wagner* (1888), he again explicitly refers to the content of his coming

---

[27] As a typical example of how Nietzsche's intention and work on this *Hauptwerk* is assumed to be irrelevant (since no such work was finished) and is associated with the problematic selection of Elisabeth and Gast, and thus, it is implied, is best ignored; see Maudemarie Clark and Alan Swensen's translation of and comments to this work (1998: 167).

Hauptwerk: 'I shall have an opportunity (in a chapter of my main work [*meines Hauptwerks*], entitled 'Toward a Physiology of Art') to show in more detail how this over-all change of art into histrionics is no less an expression of physiological degeneration' (CW 7).

Nietzsche regarded his next work, the short *Twilight of the Idols* (1888), as a summary or rather as a collection of extracts of his philosophy so far (he considered giving it the subtitle 'My Philosophy in Extract'). That this work was written in the shadow of his projected *Hauptwerk* is visible in the title, preface, general contents and the last sentence of the book as well as the last sentence of the penultimate chapter. Until the very end, the proof-reading stage of the manuscript, Nietzsche had a different and much less belligerent title for the work: *Müßiggang eines Psychologen* (*The Idle Hours of a Psychologist*), implying, as he also states in the preface, that he here takes a pause from the difficult task of writing his *Hauptwerk* – for the purpose of giving extracts of his philosophy so far. The subtitle to the new title, 'or How to Philosophize with the Hammer', is somewhat misleading and its primary meaning has not been understood by most readers. As one can see from Nietzsche's notebooks, the hammer is for him a symbol for the idea of eternal recurrence, and the title thus first and foremost means: how to philosophize from the perspective of eternal recurrence, that is, how to philosophize from the perspective of examining whether these ideas and values increase or decrease your will and ability to affirm life and reality.[28] The subtitle is in part misleading since he does not explicitly discuss the idea of eternal recurrence in the book (since he saves that for the *Hauptwerk*), but *Twilight of the Idols* consists largely of severe critique of decadence and pessimism – that is, of views that reduce the value of life and reality. On the other hand, Nietzsche felt that his thinking from 1881 onwards had been shaped by this idea, so the subtitle is perhaps not inappropriate (apart from the fact that very few of his readers could have been able to realize the primary meaning of it – at least until the fourth book of his *Hauptwerk* or the contents of his notebooks had been published).

In the preface to *Twilight of the Idols*, Nietzsche explicitly says that he is working on his *Hauptwerk*, at this late stage titled *Revaluation of All Values*:

> To stay cheerful when involved in a gloomy and exceedingly responsible business is no inconsiderable art: yet what could be more necessary than cheerfulness? Nothing succeeds in which high spirits play no part. Only excess of strength is proof of strength. – A *revaluation of all values* [or *Revaluation of All Values*], this question-mark so black, so huge it casts

---

[28] See Brobjer (1999) and (2023a).

a shadow over him who sets it up – such a destiny of a task [i.e. writing the *Hauptwerk* and revaluing values] compels one every instant to run out into the sunshine so as to shake off a seriousness grown all too oppressive. Every expedient for doing so is justified, every 'occasion' a joyful occasion [i.e., this book, as well as his previous book, *The Case of Wagner*, are welcomed pauses in that much more difficult task].

Furthermore, he ends the short preface by explicitly stating that he had just finished the first volume of the *Hauptwerk*, i.e., *The Antichrist*: 'Turin, 30 September 1888, on the day the first book of the *Revaluation of All Values* was completed.'[29]

The content of *Twilight of the Idols* is highly interesting and he allowed himself to use material and notes that he had set aside for his *Hauptwerk*, but he nonetheless – intentionally – avoided many of the themes he planned to cover in his *Hauptwerk*, such as eternal recurrence and nihilism. Other topics, such as the physiology of aesthetics, higher human beings, the revaluation of all values, and *amor fati* he only alluded to.

The last sentence of the book (with the exception of the quotation from *Thus Spoke Zarathustra* placed on a separate page at the end) – with references to revaluation of all values (the title of his *Hauptwerk*), Dionysus and eternal recurrence – surely is meant to point forward to his coming *Hauptwerk* (just as the end of *The Gay Science* promised *Thus Spoke Zarathustra*): 'the *Birth of Tragedy* was my first revaluation of all values: with that I again plant myself in the soil out of which I draw all that I will and *can* – I, the last disciple of the philosopher Dionysus – I, the teacher of the eternal recurrence ....'. This pointing forwards to his coming *Hauptwerk* is still more obvious at the end of the penultimate chapter of the book, 'Expeditions of an Untimely Man', which originally was meant to constitute the end of the book:[30] 'I have given mankind the most profound book it possesses, my *Zarathustra*: I shall shortly give it the most independent [i.e., his *Hauptwerk*].'

That *Twilight of the Idols* did not constitute the end of Nietzsche's intention to philosophize is clear from letters in which Nietzsche speaks of the book as preparatory and preparing the way for his *Hauptwerk*. In a letter to Gast, 12 September 1888 (KSB 8:1105), written immediately after having finished the manuscript, he states that: 'the book [*Twilight of the Idols*] can serve the purpose of *initiating* and *whetting the appetite* for my *Revaluation of All Values*

---

[29] Nietzsche writes the German *Umwerthung aller Werthe* in exactly the same way in the two quoted texts from the preface, while in English one is forced to choose between a statement in italics or a title.

[30] Nietzsche at a very late stage during the proofreading added the final chapter "What I Owe to the Ancients" (which actually was written for *Ecce Homo*) to the manuscript.

(which first book is almost completed)'. Two days later, he writes to Deussen (KSB 8:1111):

> My publisher already has another manuscript, which is a very stringent and subtle expression of my whole philosophical heterodoxy – hidden behind much gracefulness and mischief. It is called 'Müssiggang eines Psychologen'. In the last analysis, both these works [*The Case of Wagner* and *Twilight of the Idols*] are only recuperations in the midst of an immeasurably difficult and decisive task which, *when it is understood*, will spit humanity into two halves. Its aim and meaning is, in four words: the *revaluation of all values*.

In December 1888, just weeks before his mental collapse, after having just received the printed book, he refers to it in a letter to H. Taine, 8 December (KSB 8:1179), as: 'in relation to that which it *prepares*, almost a piece of fate', and on a postcard to Naumann, 20 December 1888 (KSB 8:1202), as 'short and in the highest degree preparatory'. That for which it was meant to be preparatory was his forthcoming *Hauptwerk*.

When Nietzsche wrote *The Antichrist* (in September 1888, although it was not published until 1895) it constituted the first volume of four of his *Hauptwerk*. This was stated, as we have seen, in the preface of *Twilight of the Idols*, as well as in the subtitle to *The Antichrist*: 'The first book of the *Revaluation of All Values*.' In the preface to the work, Nietzsche states that this book belongs to (i.e., can only be understood by) the very few, possibly those who understood his *Thus Spoke Zarathustra*, thus connecting his *Hauptwerk* to his previous masterpiece.[31] The first fourteen sections of the book are more general and say something about the overall *Hauptwerk*. He there emphasizes the importance of being willing and creating higher human beings, which so far have only been 'lucky hits'. This should be seen as a parallel to his *Übermensch*-theme in *Thus Spoke Zarathustra*. Still more importantly, in these sections, he makes a strong dichotomy between ancient (healthy) and modern and Christian (decadent) values, which much of his attempt at a revaluation relates to. By section 15, he begins to more concentrate on the main theme of the first book of his *Hauptwerk*, a revaluation of Christian values and a harsh critique of religion and Christianity.

It is surprising – and unfortunate – that these first fourteen sections have never been read and discussed as representing part of his greater *Hauptwerk*, rather than just being part of *The Antichrist*. Such an analysis (especially in combination with an examination of the late Nietzsche's notes for that work) would yield much interesting material for the direction of the late Nietzsche's thought. In section six, for example, he speaks explicitly of a theme he planned

---

[31] I have discussed of the relationship between the projected *Hauptwerk* and *Thus Spoke Zarathustra* in Brobjer (2023b).

to discuss in a volume of his *Hauptwerk* relating to his revaluation of values: 'A history of the "higher feelings", of the "ideals of mankind" – and it is possible that I shall have to narrate it – would almost also constitute an explanation of *why* man is so depraved.' There is, however, no space here for such an analysis of the contents of the beginning of *The Antichrist*.

Nietzsche decided that for his *Hauptwerk* to be read and understood, he needed to prepare the ground – and especially explain why he has been able to see what no one else has seen or realized for two thousand years – by writing his *Ecce Homo* (written in October and the first days of November, with mostly minor revisions added in late November and December 1888) and meant to be published before his *Hauptwerk* (including *The Antichrist*). Nietzsche refers to it as 'a in the highest degree preparatory text' to his *Hauptwerk* in a letter to Naumann, 6 November 1888 (KSB 8:1139), and it contains continual references to his future *Hauptwerk*. Just to mention a few examples: The very first sentence of the book announces his future work: 'Seeing that I must shortly approach mankind with the heaviest demand that ever has been made on it [i.e., the revaluation], it seems to me indispensable to say *who I am*.' At the end of the preface, as a separate paragraph, is a short text originally dated on Nietzsche's birthday, 15 October 1888, in which he again refers to *The Antichrist* as the first book of his *Hauptwerk*: 'The first book of the *Revaluation of All Values*, the *Songs of Zarathustra*, the *Twilight of the Idols*, my attempt to philosophize with the hammer – all of them gifts of this year, of its last quarter even!' When Nietzsche revised this text in November and December, he struck out the date, but – significantly – continued to refer to *The Antichrist* as the first volume of the *Hauptwerk*. When Nietzsche carefully read the manuscript of *Ecce Homo* during the first week of December – 'weighing each word on a gold scale' (letter to Gast, 9 December 1888, KSB 8:1181) – and again when he read the proofs during the middle of the month,[32] he still kept referring to *The Antichrist* as '*the first book* of the *Revaluation*' (my emphasis). He lets this description remain, although he made a number of other changes in the prologue, when he returned the proofs of the first part of *Ecce Homo* to his publisher Naumann with the words 'druckfertig / N' ('ready to print / N'), and dated by Nietzsche as 'Turin, den 18. Dez. 1888'.[33] This makes the claim that *The Antichrist* had become the complete *Revaluation of All Values* already a month earlier highly unlikely or incorrect. It is clearly stated here, and ready for publication, on

---

[32] Compare Montinari (1982: 122) "Der erste und zweite Bogen des *Ecce homo* waren von Nietzsche am 18. Dezember 1888 'Druckfertig' nach Leipzig zurückgeschickt worden." Compare Nietzsche's letter to Naumann, 18 December 1888 (KSB 8:1198).

[33] KSA 14, 459. See also the first page of the proofs which are extant.

18 December 1888, that *The Antichrist* is 'das erste Buch der *Umwerthung aller Werthe*'.[34] When Nietzsche revised his *Nietzsche contra Wagner*, which he had begun writing and compiling on 12 December, in the middle part of December (before 22 December), he then again refers to *The Antichrist* as the 'first book of the *Revaluation of Values*' in a revision of this text that he eventually did not use.[35] This again severely contradicts any claim that *The Antichrist* had become the whole *Revaluation of All Values* already in November.

The last book Nietzsche discussed in *Ecce Homo* was *The Case of Wagner*, and at the very end of the discussion, he explicitly refers to his coming *Hauptwerk*: 'And so, about two years before the shattering thunder of the *Revaluation* which will set the earth into convulsions, I sent the "Wagner Case" into the world.' He thus planned to publish the *Hauptwerk* in or near 1890. In a letter to Overbeck, 13 Nov. 1888 (KSB 8:1143), he writes: 'At the end of next year, the *first* book of the *Revaluation* will be published. It lies here finished.'

The last chapter of *Ecce Homo*, 'Why I Am a Destiny', is to a large part centred upon his coming work: '*Revaluation of All Values*: this is my formula [and also the title of his coming *Hauptwerk*] for an act of supreme coming-to-oneself on the part of mankind [. . .] I am a *bringer of good tidings* such as there has never been' (section 1).

Nietzsche's intention to write a *Hauptwerk* is still more prominent in his letters than in his published books. In them, we also get some hints as to the nature of the *Hauptwerk*. He explicitly refers to such a work as his *Hauptwerk* in a number of letters between 1886 and 1888, but an intention to write such a work is clear already from at least 1884 onwards.

Nietzsche began to feel a new and intensive sense of purpose with his 'discovery' of the idea of eternal recurrence (and other related 'discoveries'

---

[34] I have included a picture of the proofs of this page of *Ecce Homo*, with Nietzsche's handwritten comments from 18 December 1888, and with his statement that the text is now ready to be printed (with the text: "The first book of the *Revaluation of All Values*," etc.), on p. 93 of my *Nietzsche's 'Ecce Homo' and the Revaluation of All Values* (2021). According to Montinari, just days before Nietzsche's mental collapse, 30 or 31 of December 1888, he apparently sent instructions (on a not extant postcard) to his publisher to strike out the words "the first book of" and changed the text to: "The *Revaluation of All Values*, the *Songs of Zarathustra*, and, as relaxation, the *Twilight of the Idols*, my attempt to philosophize with the hammer – all of them gifts of this year, of its last quarter even!" (KSA 14, 462f).

[35] In this planned addition to *Nietzsche contra Wagner*, "Wir Antipoden," Nietzsche wrote (sometime near the middle of December): "Dieser Satz, hart und schneidig geworden unter dem Hammerschlag der historischen Erkenntniß (– lisez: erstes Buch der *Umwerthung der Werthe* –)," and so on. Montinari does not refer to it in his essay "Nietzsches Nachlaß von 1885 bis 1888 oder Textkritik und Wille zur Macht," in *Nietzsche lesen* (1982). However, as a reliable editor, he gives the text as an eventually not used addition to "Wir Antipoden" (KSA 14, 525f).

made near that time) in early August 1881. He then began to refer to his 'task', 'life-task', 'fundamental task', and 'main task' (*Aufgabe, Lebensaufgabe, Hauptsache,* and *Hauptaufgabe*), and similar expressions, and that he will require several years' time to develop it.[36]

The intention to write a *Hauptwerk* becomes explicit in five letters from the spring of 1884 where Nietzsche speaks of *Thus Spoke Zarathustra* as merely an 'entrance hall' to his philosophy, and that he was working on the main building. In the second of these letters, to Meysenbug, end of March 1884 (KSB 6:498), he writes that he has finished his *Thus Spoke Zarathustra* and thereafter calls that work 'an entrance hall to my philosophy – built for me, to give me courage', and he hints at that he is working on 'the main building'.

In three further letters, he refers to *Thus Spoke Zarathustra* as merely the 'Vorhalle' to his philosophy, and he refers to his strong sense of purpose and mission. It seems clear that he had in mind a more philosophical (and less metaphorical) work than *Thus Spoke Zarathustra*, but which, in all likelihood, would elaborate on similar fundamental ideas.

> If I get to Sils Maria in the summer, I mean to set about revising my metaphysical and epistemological views. I must now proceed step by step through a series of disciplines, for I have decided to spend the next five years on an elaboration of my 'philosophy', the entrance hall of which I have built with my *Zarathustra*. (Letter to Overbeck, 7 April 1884, KSB 6:504)

A month later, he repeats the intention to work on a *Hauptwerk*, then referred to as 'Haupt-Bau', i.e., 'main building'.

> Now, after that I for me have built this entrance hall to my philosophy, I will have to start again and not grow tired until the main building also stands finished before me. (Letter to Meysenbug, early May 1884, KSB 6:509)

In fact, this was not only an intention, for during much of 1884 Nietzsche actually planned and worked on this *Hauptwerk* or 'main building' of his philosophy. In early autumn, Nietzsche seems to confirm that he had fulfilled his plans.

> I have practically finished the main task which I set myself for this summer; the next six years will be for working out a scheme which I have sketched for my 'philosophy'. It has gone well and looks hopeful. (Letter to Gast, 2 September 1884, KSB 6:529)

---

[36] See, for example, letter to Elisabeth, 18 August 1881 (KSB 6:138), to Overbeck, 20/21 August 1881 (KSB 6:139), to Ida Overbeck, 19 January 1882 (KSB 6:188), to Gast, 3 September 1883 (KSB 6:461), and to Overbeck, 12 February 1884 (KSB 6:488).

After having finished *On the Genealogy of Morals* (summer 1887), he writes that his whole life continues to be determined by 'the nowadays completely absorbing main task [*Hauptpensum*] of my life', that is, his work on the *Hauptwerk*. During 1887 and most of 1888, Nietzsche was also intensively engaged in this work on the *Hauptwerk* as can be confirmed when one examines his notes.

It is primarily with the aid of Nietzsche's notebooks that we can see and discuss the planned contents of his *Hauptwerk*. However, already from the letters, it is clear that it was planned to be a four-volume work, which was meant to present and elaborate his thoughts in a more structured and theoretical manner than is done in any of his other books. Not only does Nietzsche refer to the planned work as a *Hauptwerk*, a 'main building', 'my lifework', "my main task", etc., suggesting, not only that it was to be a magnum opus, but also that it was going to be a more 'complete', structured, and theoretical work than his other books. It seems likely that he considered its form to be something treatise-like, perhaps akin to the essays in *On the Genealogy of Morals*.[37] Already in 1883, he speaks of wanting to construct something more 'theoretical', thereafter he refers to his *Hauptwerk* as a 'conception' as '*a coherent construction of thought*', 'my conception as a whole', that he will perform a 'working through of my 'philosophy', 'work through a scheme, with which I have outlined my "philosophy"', 'work through my complete system of thought', and in September 1888 he refers to its 'very strict and earnest character'.[38] That those descriptions are accurate is confirmed by the first volume, *The Antichrist*, which is written as a sort of polemical treatise.

The most important source of information about Nietzsche's projected *Hauptwerk* and its planned contents can be found in his notebooks.[39] It is possible to find a very large number of outlines of titles of planned books related to Nietzsche's *Hauptwerk* in them from the later 1880s. Nietzsche's work on and notes for the *Hauptwerk* 1884–88 can be divided into several periods, and during this time there are several more extensive collections of notes for, and corresponding tables of contents of, that work, but we can here concentrate on only the last one.

---

[37] Nietzsche re-read his *On the Genealogy of Morals* during July–August 1888, shortly before he wrote *The Antichrist*, and Montinari has suggested that these essays constituted a model and stimulus for how he was to write his *Umwerthung aller Werthe*. I agree that this seems likely.

[38] See letters to Gast, 3 September 1883 (KSB 6:461), Seydlitz, 17 August 1886 (KSB 7:737), to Overbeck, 24 March 1887 (KSB 8:820), to Brandes, 4 May 1888 (KSB 8:1030), to Overbeck, 7 April 1884 (KSB 6:504), to Gast, 2 September 1884 (KSB 6:529) and to Naumann, 7 September 1888 (KSB 8:1103).

[39] Here only a superficial overview of this information can be given since they cover about 1,500 printed pages in the KSA-version. Actually, in the new KGW IX-version, they cover about 4,000 pages.

The final period covers the autumn 1887 until the late autumn 1888, when he worked intensively on his projected *Hauptwerk*, but taking two resting-breaks and writing *The Case of Wagner* and *Twilight of the Idols*. He then began to use three large bound notebooks exclusively for collecting notes for his *Hauptwerk*.[40] He during the first half of this period wrote and copied down from earlier notebooks in legible handwriting a large number of notes into them, which led to over 500 notes on over 450 printed pages of notes for the project. He later returned to them, organized, and numbered 374 of them. These notes can be regarded as Nietzsche's most extensive draft for his *Hauptwerk*. This is obviously not a finished work to be published by Nietzsche, but together with his later revisions of these notes and his later notes, this constitutes an important source for anyone interested in Nietzsche's thought and philosophy.

This work on his *Hauptwerk* he refers to in a letter to Elisabeth, 15 October 1887 (KSB 8:925):

> On the other hand, there is not the slightest chance once my *magnum opus* [*mein Hauptwerk*] is finished to bring it to the world other than through 'self-print'. [. . .] Forgive me, if I due to these worries about the future (that is about making my *magnum opus* possible, in which the problem and the task of my life is concentrated) now behave in regard to financial questions with unwilling worry and hesitation.

In February 1888, he began using a new fourth notebook,[41] and filled half of it with an 'index' to the three previous notebooks, in which these notes are briefly, usually in one sentence, summarized and numbered 1–372 (the same as in the other notebooks). The first three hundred of these summaries are also attributed to the four volumes of his *Hauptwerk* by using Roman numerals. There is also a plan for the whole *Hauptwerk*, in four volumes divided into twelve chapters (KSA 13, 12[2]).[42] These notes can be regarded as Nietzsche's most extensive and consistent draft for his *Hauptwerk*. In letters to Overbeck and to Gast, from mid-February 1888, he calls this extensive collection of notes 'the first written

---

[40] "W II 1" (KSA 12, 9), "W II 2" (KSA 12, 10), and "W II 3" (KSA 13, 11). These are large hardcover notebooks. The contents of them have been published in facsimile and diplomatic transcription in KGW IX.6 and IX.7.

[41] "W II 4" (KSA 13, 12[1 and 2]), a bound notebook of originally 127 pages. Used as "index" for the three notebooks "W II 1, 2, 3" (listing with a one-line summary of each of the numbered notes intended for use in his *Hauptwerk*) on sixty handwritten pages in the notebook and in the 17-page -long note KSA 13, 12[1], written in February 1888. As with almost all of the notebooks, Nietzsche wrote in them from back to front. In this notebook, about twenty pages have been ripped or cut out – possibly because Nietzsche wanted to use the notes somewhere else (?). Between the "index," 12[1], which is written on every second page, and the table of contents of the four books of the *Hauptwerk*, 12[2], there are a fairly large number of pages and cut out pages, not visible in KSA 13.

[42] This note is published in diplomatic transcription in KGW IX.7, W II 4, p. 4.

version of my 'Umwerthung aller Werthe' is finished'.[43] We can also note that already at this time, in several letters, he refers to his *Hauptwerk* as the *Revaluation of All Values* rather than as *The Will to Power.*

Nietzsche extensively worked through and revised many of the full 374 notes again in the summer of 1888, that is, just before he wrote *Twilight of the Idols* and *The Antichrist*, and later some of them, but much less than ten per cent of them, he used for writing these two books (and usually he then struck the note out – not visible in KSA). However, the great majority of these notes were certainly not discarded.

Examining these notes and notebooks, we are looking into Nietzsche's workshop. Many English-language philosophers use only the texts in Nietzsche's published books, and simply disregard his notes and regard them as 'discarded material'. This is false and sad indeed, and a reflection that they have never visited 'Nietzsche's workshop' and seen how intensively he developed and worked with his ideas and texts.

This collection of notes can be used as a reasonable starting point for an attempt to provisionally construct the contents of the four volumes of the *Umwerthung aller Werthe*. Furthermore, we know that Nietzsche returned to this collection of notes at least four times after February 1888, and revised and added to them, obviously because he continued to regard them as valid. Even more important is that we know that he used them in and for drafting large part of his work on the first volume of the *Umwerthung aller Werthe*, *The Antichrist*, in September 1888. In a note, from September 1888, KSA 13, 22[2], Nietzsche is drafting major parts of *The Antichrist* (covering material discussed in sections 41–55 of the finished *The Antichrist*). This is the only extant note in which he drafts the contents of major parts of *The Antichrist*. He there explicitly uses his 'index' from February 1888 (KSA 13, 12[1], where he had summarized the 374 notes that he had written for the *Umwerthung aller Werthe*), and adds where ten of these notes should be added to the text. Some of the other brief texts in the note seem also to have been created from this selection of notes.[44] He thus obviously still regarded this selection of notes and summaries as valid in September 1888, and as a useful source of stimulus, notes, and information, and it seems likely that it can, with some care, also be used for information about the planned contents of the further three volumes.

---

[43] In letters to Overbeck and to Gast, both dated 13 February 1888 (KSB 8:990 and 991): "die erste Niederschrift meiner 'Umwertung aller Werthe' ist fertig." In the letter to Gast he expresses it similarly: "Ich habe die erste Niederschrift meines 'Versuchs einer Umwertung' fertig."

[44] He had done likewise, in his earlier outline of the *Hauptwerk* (for what seems to be volume 1 about nihilism and truth in three chapters, in May–June 1888, that later becomes volume 2), KSA 13, 17[1], from May 1888, which also contains seven references to that index and these 374 notes.

Furthermore, we know which notes of the 300 are allocated to which volumes (but not to which chapters Nietzsche intended them, with a few exceptions). In one note, where he takes an overview of the whole project, he plans 50 pages per chapter and thus 150 pages per volume (KSA 13, 13[4], from the early part of 1888), and we can see that the attributed full notes in notebooks W II 1–3 constitute a substantial working material for writing such chapters.

During September, Nietzsche in several letters expressed his optimism and sense of achievement, but thereafter, in November and December 1888, there were few notes and none of them philosophical. These last two months before the collapse, Nietzsche was busy writing, editing, correcting, proofreading a number of works, including *Ecce Homo*, and he wrote well over a hundred letters. However, that which prevented the completion of the *Hauptwerk* was, in my view, apart from the mental collapse, less that he was busy, but more that there was no hurry. He had decided to write, finish, and publish *Ecce Homo* before and as preparatory, and thus the work on the *Hauptwerk* could and had to wait. Still more important were the signs of mental instability during these two last months, visible especially in his letters. We have no evidence that he consciously decided to give up the plan for a *Hauptwerk*. Between 1881 and 1885, there are many different titles used, but from the summer of 1885, there are only two, used consecutively, first *Will to Power* and then *Revaluation of All Values*, the latter that earlier had been the subtitle to the former.

2.4 The Planned Contents of the *Revaluation of All Values*

We will in this section examine and summarize Nietzsche's plans for the *Hauptwerk* on two levels. First by briefly reviewing his plans for the title of the work (summarized in Table 1), thereafter the planned titles of the four books or volumes and their planned chapter titles (summarized in Table 2). One could go further and discuss the very large number of extant notes explicitly written for the *Hauptwerk* among his notebooks but there is no space for that here.[45] Many of the late notes discussing themes planned to be discussed in the future three volumes of the *Hauptwerk*, such as truth, nihilism, immoralism, and eternal recurrence are highly relevant and need to be examined not as discarded texts but as working material for Nietzsche's last unfinished project.

There are a very large number of drafts of titles for the *Hauptwerk* project in Nietzsche's notebooks, far more than for any other projected or realized book. There are good reasons to regard these different titles as referring to essentially the same planned *Hauptwerk*.

---

[45] I have done a partial such study in my book *The Close Relationship between Nietzsche's Two Most Important Books* (2023b).

Table 1 The evolution of the planned titles of Nietzsche's magnum opus, from autumn 1881 to December 1888

Autumn 1881– Summer 1885	→	Aug. 1885–Aug. 1888	→	Sept.–Dec. 1888
3–5 books (but mostly 4)		Consisting of 4 books		4 books
Many different titles		Consistent title		Consistent title (earlier subtitle)
Not called *Hauptwerk*, but,		Called *Hauptwerk*		Called *Hauptwerk*
e.g., 'Haupt-Bau' (in 1884)				
The New Order of Rank The Eternal Recurrence Philosophy of Eternal Recurrence Midday and Eternity The Innocence of Becoming Dionysus Philosophy of the Future	}	The Will to Power	→	Revaluation of All Values

We can get much further information by examining the titles of the planned four books, and the chapters they were planned to contain. When we limit ourselves to the final situation, from September 1888 onwards, we can observe that we possess seven drafts for or lists of titles of the books of the *Umwerthung aller Werthe*, from after he began writing *The Antichrist*, all very similar.[46] However, these contain no listing of chapter titles, as some of the earlier listings do. Using the consistent divisions into four books after that *The Antichrist* was decided upon; we can go back to the more detailed divisions from earlier in 1888 and classify these chapter titles according to these new book divisions. It turns out that this is relatively straightforward using the three most detailed chapter divisions. This information is presented in Table 2 and gives us a reasonably detailed view of Nietzsche's plans for the three remaining volumes of the *Umwerthung aller Werthe*.

---

[46] KSA 13, 19[2 and 8], 11[416], 22[14 and 24], and 23[8 and 13].

Table 2 Planned Chapter Titles for Nietzsche's *Hauptwerk* from earlier in 1888, here classified and organized according to the book divisions from September to December 1888

Unwerthung aller Werthe Sept.–Dec. 1888	**Table of contents from early 1888**	**Table of contents from May or June of 1888**	**Table of contents from 26 August 1888**
	KSA 13, 12[2]	KSA 13, 16[51]	KSA 13, 18[17]
Book 1			
The Anti-Christ: Attempt at a Critique of Christianity	*Critique of the Christian ideals*	The *religious* man as typical décadent	The homines religiosi
		The pagan in religion	Thoughts about Christianity
Book 2			
The Free Spirit: Critique of Philosophy as a Nihilistic Movement	*Nihilism, considered to its final conclusion*	The true and the apparent world	The psychology of errors
	'Will to truth'	The philosopher as typical décadent	The value of truth and error
	Culture, Civilization, the ambivalence of the 'modern'	Science against philosophy	The will to truth
		Nihilism [and its opposite]	The metaphysicians
			To the history of European nihilism

Table 2 (cont.)

Umwerthung aller Werthe	Table of contents from early 1888	Table of contents from May or June of 1888	Table of contents from 26 August 1888
Book 3			
The Immoralist: Critique of Morality as the Most Dangerous Kind of Lack of Knowledge	*The origin of ideals* *How virtue becomes victorious* *Herd-instincts* *Morality as the Circe of the philosophers* *Psychology of the 'will to power'*	The *good* human being as typical décadent	The good and the improvers
Book 4			
Dionysus: The Philosophy of Eternal Recurrence	*Life-prescriptions for us* *'Eternal recurrence'* *Great politics*	The will to power as life: Peak of the historical *self-consciousness* The will to power: as discipline	*The principle of life: 'Order of rank'* *The two ways* *The eternal recurrence*

It is further possible to get a much more detailed view of how Nietzsche envisaged the contents of the *Umwerthung aller Werthe* by using the 374 numbered notes in the notebooks W II 1–4 and placing them into Table 2, or into a similar structure. Such a scheme can be further improved by including notes written for the *Hauptwerk* in the following notebooks, W II 5–8. However, there is no room for such detailed treatment here.

Notes on Texts, Translations, and Abbreviations

The following abbreviations and translations of Nietzsche's works are used in this volume. In the references to Nietzsche's works, Roman numerals generally denote the volume number of a set of collected works or the standard subdivision within a single work, and Arabic numerals denote the relevant section number. 'Pref' is the abbreviation for the preface to a given work (except for the preface to the 1886 edition of *The Birth*). Page numbers are added when sections are long, providing more precise information about the location of the relevant text. In citing Nietzsche's notes in KGW and KSA, references provide the volume number (and part for KGW) followed by the relevant fragment number. The one exception is KSA 14, in which case the page number is provided. In citing KGB, these numbers are given as well as the relevant letter number (same as in KSB). Corresponding references to *The Will to Power* (WP) will be given only when deemed important to do so. In citing KSB, the volume number is followed by the number of the letter.

Abbreviations for Nietzsche's Collected Works in the Original German

KGW   *Friedrich Nietzsche: Werke. Kritische Gesamtausgabe.* Edition founded by G. Colli and M. Montinari, continued by V. Gerhardt, N. Miller, W. Müller-Lauter and K. Pestalozzi. Berlin, NY: Walter de Gruyter (1967ff.).

KSA   *Friedrich Nietzsche: Sämtliche Werke. Kritische Studienausgabe*, eds. G. Colli and M. Montinari, 15 vols. Berlin: De Grutyer (1999).

KSB   *Friedrich Nietzsche: Sämtliche Briefe. Kritische Studienausgabe*, eds. G. Colli and M. Montinari, 8 vols. Berlin: Walter de Gruyter (1986).

Quoted texts from Nietzsche's letters and notes have been translated by me, unless otherwise stated.

Abbreviations and Translations for Titles of Published Works*

BGE   *Jenseits von Gut und Böse* (1886): translated as *Beyond Good and Evil*. In *Beyond Good and Evil*, trans. R. J. Hollingdale. London: Penguin (1990).

---

* Dates are years of publication.

BT   *Die Geburt der Tragödie* (1872/1886); translated as *The Birth of Tragedy*. In *The Birth of Tragedy and the Case of Wagner*, trans. W. Kaufmann, 15–151. New York: Vintage (1967). The 'Attempt at a Self-Criticism' added to the 1886 edition is cited as 'ASC' followed by the relevant section number.

CW   *Der Fall Wagner* (1888); translated as *The Case of Wagner*. In *The Birth of Tragedy and the Case of Wagner*, trans. W. Kaufmann, 153–192. New York: Vintage (1967).

D   *Morgenröthe* (1881/1887); translated as *Daybreak*. In *Daybreak*, ed. M. Clark and B. Leiter, trans. R. J. Hollingdale. Cambridge: Cambridge University Press (1997).

GM   *Zur Genealogie der Moral* (1887); translated as *On the Genealogy of Morals*. In *On the Genealogy of Morals and Ecce Homo*, trans. W. Kaufmann, 13–163. New York: Random House (1989).

GS   *Die fröhliche Wissenschaft* (1882/1887); translated as *The Gay Science*. In *The Gay Science*, trans. W. Kaufmann. New York: Vintage Books (1974).

HH   *Menschliches, Allzumenschliches* (1878/1886); translated as *Human, All Too Human*. In *Human, All Too Human*, trans. R. J. Hollingdale, 5–205. Cambridge: Cambridge University Press (1996). References to the two-volume 1886 edition are indicated by Roman numerals (*HH* I and *HH* II).

SE   *Schopenhauer als Erzieher* (*Unzeitgemässe Betrachtungen* III) (1874); translated as *Schopenhauer as Educator* (*Untimely Meditation* IV). In *Untimely Meditations*, ed. D. Breazeale, trans. R. J. Hollingdale, 125–194. Cambridge: Cambridge University Press (1997).

TI   *Götzen-Dämmerung* (1888); translated as *Twilight of the Idols*. In *Twilight of the Idols and the Anti-Christ*, trans. R. J. Hollingdale. London: Penguin (1990). References include an abbreviated chapter title and section number.

UM   *Unzeitgemässe Betrachtungen* (1873–1876); translated as *Untimely Meditations*. In *Untimely Meditations*, ed. D. Breazeale, trans. R. J. Hollingdale. Cambridge: Cambridge University Press (1997).

Z   *Also sprach Zarathustra* (1883–1885; part IV was only distributed privately during Nietzsche's lifetime); translated as *Thus Spoke Zarathustra*. In *Thus Spoke Zarathustra*, trans. G. Parkes. Oxford: Oxford University Press (2005). References include part number (I–IV), abbreviated chapter title, and section number if relevant.

Abbreviations and Translations for Private Publications, Authorized Manuscripts, and Unpublished Works**

A   *Der Antichrist* (1888); translated as *The Antichrist*. In *Twilight of the Idols and the Anti-Christ*, trans. R. J. Hollingdale. London: Penguin (1990).

EH   *Ecce homo* (1888); translated as *Ecce Homo*. In *Ecce Homo*, trans. R. J. Hollingdale. London: Penguin (1980). References include abbreviated chapter title and section number; in the chapter 'Books', the section number is preceded by the abbreviation of the relevant book title.

Abbreviations and Translations for Nietzsche's Unpublished Notebooks

WP   *Der Wille zur Macht* (1883–1888); translated as *The Will to Power*. In *The Will to Power*, ed. W. Kaufmann, trans. W. Kaufmann and R. J. Hollingdale. New York: Vintage (1968). *Der Wille zur Macht* was originally put together from Nietzsche's notes by E. Förster-Nietzsche and Peter Gast in 1901, with an enlarged second edition in 1906.

** Dates are years of composition.

References

Ackermann, Robert J. (1989). *Nietzsche: A Frenzied Look*. Amherst: University of Massachusetts Press.

Brobjer, Thomas H. (1999). 'Götzen-Hammer: The Meaning of the Expression "to Philosophize with a Hammer"'. *Nietzsche-Studien* 28: 38–41.

(2003). 'Nietzsche's Affirmative Morality: An Ethics of Virtue'. *Journal of Nietzsche Studies* 26: 64–78.

(2008). *Nietzsche's Philosophical Context: An Intellectual Biography*. Urbana: University of Illinois Press.

(2021). *Nietzsche's 'Ecce Homo' and the Revaluation of All Values: Dionysian versus Christian Values*. London: Bloomsbury Academic.

(2023a). *Twilight of the Idols and Nietzsche's Late Philosophy: Toward a Revaluation of Values*. London: Bloomsbury Academic.

(2023b). *The Close Relationship between Nietzsche's Two Most Important Books*. London: Palgrave Macmillan.

Cate, Curtis (2002). *Friedrich Nietzsche*. London: Hutchinson.

Deussen, Paul (1883). *Das System des Vedânta*. Leipzig: F. A. Brockhaus.

Foot, Philippa (1973). 'Nietzsche: The Revaluation of Values'. In Solomon (1973, 1980), 156–168.

Gilman, Sander L. (1981). *Begegnungen mit Nietzsche*. Bonn: Bouvier Verlag.

Higgins, Kathleen (1987). *Nietzsche's Zarathustra*. Philadelphia, PA: Temple University Press.

Historisches Wörterbuch der Philosophie, Band 12 (2004) Basel: Schwabe.

(2006). 'Rebaptizing our Evil: On the Revaluation of All Values'. In *A Companion to Nietzsche*, Keith Ansell Pearson, ed., 404–418. Malden, MA: Blackwell Publishing.

Hollingdale, Reginald J. (1999). *Nietzsche: The Man and His Philosophy*. 1965, reprinted with additions 1999. Cambridge: Cambridge University Press.

Huang, Jing (2019). 'Did Nietzsche Want His Notes Burned? Some Reflections on the *Nachlass* Problem'. *British Journal of the History of Philosophy* 27: 1194–1214.

Janz, Curt Paul (1993). *Friedrich Nietzsche: Biographie*, 3 vols. 1978, second revised edition 1993. München: Carl Hanser Verlag.

Jaspers, Karl (1985). *Nietzsche: An Introduction to the Understanding of His Philosophical Activity*, trans. C. F. Wallraff and F. J. Schmitz. New York: University Press of America.

Kaufmann, Walter (1974). *Nietzsche: Philosopher, Psychologist, Antichrist* (fourth ed.). Princeton, NJ: Princeton University Press.

Kissling, Beat (1992). *Die Umwertung der Werte als pädagogisches Projekt Nietzsches*. Doctoral dissertation. University of Konstanz.

Kranak, Joseph (2014). *Nietzsche's Revaluation of All Values*. Doctoral dissertation. Marquette University.

Large, Duncan (1998). 'Introduction' to His Translation of *Twilight of the Idols, Oxford World's Classics*. Oxford: Oxford University Press.

Magnus, Bernd (1986). 'Nietzsche's Philosophy in 1888: *The Will to Power* and the *Übermensch*'. *Journal of the History of Philosophy* 24: 79–98.

(1988). 'The Deification of the Commonplace: Twilight of the Idol'. In *Reading Nietzsche*, R. Solomon and K. Higgins (eds.), 152–181.

May, Keith M. (1990). *Nietzsche and the Spirit of Tragedy*. London: Macmillan.

Meyer, Matthew (2014). *Reading Nietzsche through the Ancients*. Berlin, NY: Walter de Gruyter.

(2024). *The Routledge Guidebook to Nietzsche's Thus Spoke Zarathustra*. London: Routledge.

Montinari, Mazzino (1982). 'Nietzsches Nachlaß von 1885 bis 1888 oder Textkritik und Wille zur Macht'. In *Montinari's Nietzsche lesen*, 92–119. Berlin, New York: Walter de Gruyter.

Nietzsche, Friedrich (1998). *On the Genealogy of Morality*, translated with comments by M. Clark and A. Swensen. Indianapolis: Hackett Publishing Company.

Nietzsche-Handbuch (2000). Stuttgart: Verlag J. B. Metzler.

Nietzsche-Lexikon(2009). Edited by Christian Niemeyer. Darmstadt: WGB.

Oldenberg, Hermann (1881). *Buddha, Sein Leben, seine Lehre, seine Gemeinde*. Berlin: W. Hertz.

Owen, David (2007). *Nietzsche's Genealogy of Morals*. Stocksfield: Acumen.

Prideaux, Sue (2018). *I Am Dynamite*. London: Faber and Faber.

Rattner, Josef (2000). *Nietzsche: Leben – Werk – Wirkung*. Würzburg: Könighausen und Neumann.

Reginster, Bernard (2006). *The Affirmation of Life*. Cambridge, MA: Harvard University Press.

Richardson, John (2004). *Nietzsche's New Darwinism*. Oxford: Oxford University Press.

(2020). *Nietzsche's Values*. Oxford: Oxford University Press.

Ridley, Aron (2005). 'Nietzsche and the Re-evaluation of Values'. *Proceedings of the Aristotelian Society* 105: 155–175.

Ross, Werner (1980). *Der ängsliche Adler*. München: dtv.

Safranski, Rüdiger (2000). *Nietzsche: Biographie seines Denkens*. München: Hanser Verlag.

Schacht, Richard (1983). *Nietzsche*. London: Routledge and Kegan Paul.

Schrift, Alan D. (2011). 'Nietzsche's *Nachlass*'. In *A Companion to Friedrich Nietzsche*, P. Bishop (ed.), 405–430. London: Camden House.

Schutte, Ofelia (1986). *Beyond Nihilism: Nietzsche without Masks*. Chicago: The University of Chicago Press.

Sleinis, Edgar E. (1994). *Nietzsche's Revaluation of Values: A Study in Strategies*. Urbana: University of Illinois Press.

Solomon, Robert C. (1973). *Nietzsche: A Collection of Critical Essays*. Notre Dame, IN: University of Notre Dame Press.

Solomon, Robert C. and Higgins, K. eds. (1988). *Reading Nietzsche*. Oxford: Oxford University Press.

Sommer, Andreas Urs (2000). *Friedrich Nietzsches 'Der Antichrist': Ein philosophisch-historischer Kommentar*. Basel: Schwabe.

Strong, Tracy B. (1988). *Friedrich Nietzsche and the Politics of Transfiguration*. Expanded Edition. Berkeley: University of California Press.

Thiele, Leslie P. (1990). *Friedrich Nietzsche and the Politics of the Soul: A Study of Heroic Individualism*. Princeton, NJ: Princeton University Press.

Würzbach, Friedrich (1969). *Umwertung aller Werte: Aus dem Nachlass zusammengestellt und herausgegeben*. München: Hanser Verlag.

Young, Julian (2010). *A Philosophical Biography: Friedrich Nietzsche*. Cambridge: Cambridge University Press.

For Anna

Cambridge Elements ≡

Philosophy of Friedrich Nietzsche

Kaitlyn Creasy

California State University, San Bernardino

Kaitlyn Creasy is Associate Professor of Philosophy at California State University, San Bernardino. She is the author of *The Problem of Affective Nihilism in Nietzsche* (2020) as well as several articles in nineteenth-century philosophy and moral psychology.

Matthew Meyer

The University of Scranton

Matthew Meyer is Professor of Philosophy at The University of Scranton. He is the author of three monographs: *Reading Nietzsche through the Ancients: An Analysis of Becoming, Perspectivism, and The Principle of Non-Contradiction* (2014), *Nietzsche's Free Spirit Works: A Dialectical Reading* (Cambridge, 2019), and *The Routledge Guidebook to Thus Spoke Zarathustra* (2024). He has also co-edited, with Paul Loeb, *Nietzsche's Metaphilosophy: The Nature, Method, and Aims of Philosophy* (Cambridge, 2019).

About the Series

Friedrich Nietzsche is one of the most important and influential philosophers of the nineteenth century. This Cambridge Elements series offers concise and structured overviews of a range of central topics in his thought, written by a diverse group of experts with a variety of approaches.

Cambridge Elements ☰

Philosophy of Friedrich Nietzsche

Elements in the Series

Printed in the United States
by Baker & Taylor Publisher Services